PATH TO PURPOSEFUL LEADERSHIP

ELEVATE YOUR IMPACT, AMPLIFY YOUR TEAM

SCOTT E. SALSBURY

Copyright © [2024] by Scott e Salsbury

All rights reserved. No part of this book may be reproduced, stored in a retrieval system, or transmitted in any form or by any means, electronic, mechanical, photocopying, recording, or otherwise, without the prior written permission of the publisher, except for brief quotations used in reviews or scholarly works.

Disclaimer: The information provided in this book is intended for educational and informational purposes only. The author and publisher are not engaged in rendering professional services. Readers are advised to seek professional guidance specific to their circumstances. Feel free to modify the details to fit the specific needs of your book.

TABLE OF CONTENTS

INTRODUCTION   4
- UNDERSTANDING PURPOSEFUL LEADERSHIP   10
- THE IMPORTANCE OF MEANINGFUL LEADERSHIP IN TODAY'S WORKPLACE   15

CHAPTER   19
1   19
FOUNDATIONS OF PURPOSEFUL LEADERSHIP   19
- DEFINING YOUR LEADERSHIP PHILOSOPHY   23
- THE ROLE OF SELF-AWARENESS   34
- CULTIVATING A GROWTH MINDSET   46

CHAPTER   63
2   63
BUILDING HIGH-PERFORMING TEAMS   63
- CREATING A CULTURE OF TRUST AND COLLABORATION   66
- EFFECTIVE COMMUNICATION STRATEGIES   79

EMPOWERING TEAM MEMBERS   91

CHAPTER   102
3   102
LEADING WITH PURPOSE AND IMPACT   102
- ESTABLISHING A PURPOSE-DRIVEN CULTURE   104

    MOTIVATING AND INSPIRING OTHERS   117
    NAVIGATING CHANGE AND CHALLENGES 131

CHAPTER 4   **147**

PERSONAL GROWTH AND CONTINUOUS IMPROVEMENT   **148**

    DEVELOPING YOUR LEADERSHIP SKILLS 152

    MENTORSHIP AND NETWORKING   165

    MEASURING YOUR IMPACT   179

CONCLUSION   **189**

    REFLECTING ON YOUR LEADERSHIP JOURNEY   193

    THE ONGOING PATH TO PURPOSEFUL LEADERSHIP   197

INTRODUCTION

True leadership is not about the position you hold, but the purpose you inspire. Discover your journey in 'Path to Purposeful Leadership' and unlock the leader within.Leadership is not defined by authority, but by the impact you make.

In 'Path to Purposeful Leadership,' embark on a transformative journey that reveals how vision, empathy, and integrity can elevate your influence. Learn to lead with purpose, inspire with passion, and create a legacy that empowers others to follow in your footsteps. Your path to becoming a leader of significance starts here.

In a bustling city where ambition often overshadowed integrity, a young woman named Maya found herself at a crossroads in her career. After years of climbing the corporate ladder, she landed a managerial position at a prestigious marketing firm. It appeared to be a dream come true at first.

Yet, deep down, she felt unfulfilled and disconnected from her team, who often worked late into the night, driven by deadlines rather than a shared vision.

One evening, while cleaning out her late grandmother's attic, Maya stumbled upon an old journal. Its pages were filled with her grandmother's thoughts on leadership, service, and community.

The words resonated with Maya, igniting a spark of inspiration. Her grandmother had always believed that true leadership was about the impact one had on others, not the titles one held. With newfound clarity, Maya realized she needed to redefine her leadership style.

Determined to lead with purpose, Maya set out to learn more about transformative leadership. She immersed herself in books, attended workshops, and connected with mentors who embodied the values she aspired to uphold. It became clear that leadership wasn't just about managing tasks; it was about cultivating an environment where everyone felt valued and inspired.

Back at work, Maya initiated a team-building retreat, encouraging open conversations about values, goals, and personal aspirations. She listened attentively as her team shared their dreams and concerns.

Through these discussions, Maya uncovered the potential within each member, recognizing that their diverse backgrounds and experiences were the keys to innovative solutions.

As months passed, a remarkable transformation unfolded within the team. The once-silent voices began to resonate with confidence, and collaboration flourished. Inspired by Maya's commitment to purpose, they started taking ownership of their projects, leading to a surge in creativity and productivity.

One day, Maya received an invitation to present their latest campaign at a major industry conference. As she stood before the audience, she shared not just the campaign's success, but also the journey of her team's collective growth.

She spoke passionately about the importance of purpose-driven leadership, emphasizing that true influence comes from empowering others.

By the end of her presentation, the room erupted in applause. Attendees approached her, eager to learn how they could implement similar changes in their organizations. Maya realized that her journey was no longer just about her career; it was about inspiring others to embrace their own paths of purposeful leadership.

Years later, as she looked back on her career, Maya felt a deep sense of fulfillment. She had not only built a successful marketing firm but had also cultivated a community of leaders who understood that their influence extended beyond themselves.

They were creating a legacy of empowerment, compassion, and integrity—one that would resonate through generations.

Maya's story exemplified the truth that leadership is not defined by authority, but by the purpose one inspires in others. She had transformed from a manager into a leader of significance, paving the way for countless others to follow in her footsteps. Through her journey, she had discovered that the path to purposeful leadership was not a destination, but a continuous journey of growth and impact.

UNDERSTANDING PURPOSEFUL LEADERSHIP

Purposeful leadership isn't just about giving orders; it's about guiding others with vision and heart, helping them see their own potential along the way. Purposeful leadership is not about commanding the path, but about illuminating it for others.

In a small village, the people faced a severe drought that threatened their crops and livelihoods. The village elder, known for her wisdom and purpose, called a meeting. Instead of simply instructing the villagers on what to do, she shared her vision of a thriving community where everyone contributed to finding a solution.

With her guidance, the villagers brainstormed and decided to work together to create an irrigation system. She led by example, helping to dig trenches and gather resources, demonstrating her commitment to the cause. As they toiled, her unwavering belief in their collective strength inspired others to contribute their skills and knowledge.

Through purposeful leadership, the elders not only addressed the immediate crisis but also united the villagers, fostering a sense of community and shared purpose that would last for generations. The village not only survived the drought but flourished, all thanks to the elder's ability to illuminate a clear path forward.

Purposeful leadership is a leadership approach centered around guiding teams and organizations with clear intention and a strong sense of mission. Unlike conventional leadership, which often focuses on short-term goals and immediate results, purposeful leadership looks beyond profit or performance metrics. It emphasizes creating a shared vision that inspires and motivates everyone involved.

At the heart of purposeful leadership is the ability to operate based on deeply held values. These values shape decision-making and behavior, ensuring that leaders remain true to their principles while leading others.

Purposeful leaders are driven by empathy and a genuine concern for their team members, understanding that emotional intelligence is key to fostering a culture of trust and collaboration. By prioritizing open communication, purposeful leaders engage in meaningful dialogue that makes their vision accessible and relatable to the entire organization.

This approach also nurtures a commitment to growth—not only for the organization but also for each individual within it. Purposeful leaders encourage continuous learning and the pursuit of personal and professional development, believing that the success of the team is intricately linked to the growth of its members. They create environments where employees feel valued and connected to a larger cause, which enhances engagement and satisfaction.

The impact of purposeful leadership is far-reaching. Teams led by such leaders tend to be more motivated, collaborative, and resilient in the face of challenges.

When everyone understands how their efforts contribute to a larger purpose, they are more likely to take initiative, work together effectively, and stay committed even when obstacles arise. This sense of purpose also fosters a positive and inclusive organizational culture, where innovation thrives because individuals feel safe to take risks and share ideas.

Purposeful leadership is about leading with authenticity and aligning actions with a clear and inspiring vision. It's not just about achieving goals, but about creating a meaningful impact that resonates with both leaders and their teams.

As the world continues to change, the relevance of purposeful leadership will only increase, making it a critical element of effective leadership in the future.

THE IMPORTANCE OF MEANINGFUL LEADERSHIP IN TODAY'S WORKPLACE

Meaningful leadership transcends mere management; it is the art of weaving purpose into the fabric of daily work. When leaders illuminate a shared vision and nurture genuine connections, they empower individuals to rise beyond their roles, fostering a culture of innovation and resilience.

In such environments, every challenge becomes an opportunity for growth, and every achievement is celebrated as a collective victory. Ultimately, a leader's greatest legacy is not just the success they achieve, but the lives they touch and the purpose they instill in the hearts of those they lead.

True leadership is not about authority, but about inspiring others to find purpose in their journey, transforming workplaces into communities where every contribution ignites collective passion and success.

In today's workplace, meaningful leadership is more crucial than ever. Leaders are not just tasked with driving results; they are responsible for cultivating a sense of purpose and direction within their teams.

Purposeful leadership goes beyond mere management; it inspires individuals to connect their personal goals with the organization's mission. This alignment fosters a deeper level of engagement, commitment, and motivation.

A leader with a clear sense of purpose sets a powerful example, creating a culture where every team member feels valued and understands how their contributions matter. Such leaders prioritize empathy, authenticity, and transparency, building trust and respect within their teams.

This creates a positive environment where employees are encouraged to innovate, collaborate, and take ownership of their work. In challenging times, a purpose-driven leader provides stability and a vision that guides the team through uncertainty.

They focus on long-term success and sustainable practices, ensuring that the organization's actions are aligned with its core values. This approach not only boosts morale and productivity but also enhances the organization's reputation and ability to attract top talent.

meaningful leadership transforms workplaces into communities where people are not just working for a paycheck but are part of something larger than themselves. It is this sense of shared purpose that drives exceptional performance, loyalty, and fulfillment, paving the way for a more resilient and successful organization.

CHAPTER

I

FOUNDATIONS OF PURPOSEFUL LEADERSHIP

True leadership flourishes where vision inspires, authenticity builds trust, and empowerment unlocks potential. Purposeful leadership is essential in today's dynamic and complex environments, emphasizing that effective leaders guide their teams toward achieving goals while also inspiring and empowering them to contribute meaningfully.

A key aspect of this leadership style is having a clear vision and articulating a compelling purpose that aligns with both organizational goals and individual aspirations. Purposeful leaders communicate this vision effectively, ensuring that team members understand their roles in contributing to it.

Authenticity plays a crucial role in building trust. Purposeful leaders are genuine, transparent, and self-aware, acknowledging their strengths and weaknesses. This authenticity fosters an environment where team members feel safe to express themselves and take risks.

Alongside authenticity, empowerment is vital; it involves equipping team members with the resources, autonomy, and support needed to make decisions. By encouraging collaboration, creativity, and accountability, purposeful leaders allow individuals to take ownership of their work and grow professionally.

Emotional intelligence is another cornerstone of purposeful leadership. It includes the capacity to identify, comprehend, and control feelings—one's own as well as those of others. Leaders who possess emotional intelligence can foster strong relationships, navigate conflicts, and create a positive organizational culture.

Ethical decision-making is paramount. Purposeful leaders prioritize ethical considerations in their choices, modeling integrity and accountability while ensuring their actions align with the organization's values and mission.

A commitment to continuous learning is also essential. Purposeful leaders encourage personal and professional development, actively seeking feedback and reflecting on their experiences. This mindset enhances their capabilities and inspires their teams to pursue growth.

Inclusivity and diversity are equally important, as purposeful leadership recognizes the value of diverse perspectives. Leaders create inclusive environments where all voices are heard and respected, enriching decision-making and fostering innovation.

Resilience is crucial in purposeful leadership. The ability to adapt and thrive in the face of challenges is a defining trait of these leaders. They model resilience by demonstrating a positive attitude, perseverance, and a willingness to learn from setbacks, encouraging their teams to do the same.

The foundations of purposeful leadership intertwine to create a supportive and productive environment. By focusing on vision, authenticity, empowerment, emotional intelligence, ethical decision-making, continuous learning, inclusivity, and resilience, leaders inspire their teams to achieve not just organizational success but also personal fulfillment.

Purposeful leadership fosters a culture where everyone can contribute their best, paving the way for sustainable growth and positive impact.

DEFINING YOUR LEADERSHIP PHILOSOPHY

Leadership is not a title, but a philosophy shaped by values, vision, and the courage to grow. It is the art of guiding others through shared purpose, fostering an environment of trust, and embracing the journey of continuous improvement.

A true leader inspires with integrity, acts with empathy, and empowers others to reach their potential, knowing that the impact of their guidance extends far beyond the moment.

Defining your leadership philosophy is a vital step on the path to purposeful leadership. It serves as a personal framework that guides your decisions, behaviors, and interactions with others.

A well-articulated leadership philosophy reflects your values, beliefs, and experiences, shaping how you lead and influence those around you.

To begin, self-reflection is essential. Consider the principles that resonate with you deeply. What motivates you as a leader? Understanding your core values will help you identify what you stand for.

This might include integrity, empathy, innovation, or collaboration. Reflecting on past experiences—both positive and negative—can also provide insights into the type of leader you aspire to be.

Engaging with others is another crucial aspect. Seek feedback from colleagues, mentors, and team members. Their perspectives can illuminate your strengths and areas for growth, enriching your understanding of effective leadership. Listening to diverse viewpoints helps you craft a philosophy that not only aligns with your vision but also resonates with those you lead.

As you develop your philosophy, articulate it clearly. Write down your beliefs about leadership and the impact you wish to have. This written statement can serve as a constant reminder of your purpose and principles, guiding you in moments of uncertainty.

Share your philosophy with your team, fostering transparency and creating a shared understanding of your leadership approach.

Living your philosophy is where the real challenge lies. Purposeful leadership requires consistency between your beliefs and actions. This means making decisions that align with your values, even when faced with difficult choices. It's about modeling the behaviors you expect from others, creating a culture of accountability and trust within your team.

Continuously revisiting and refining your leadership philosophy is also important. As you gain new experiences and insights, your beliefs may evolve. Embrace this growth, allowing your philosophy to adapt and remain relevant in an ever-changing landscape.

Defining your leadership philosophy is a journey of self-discovery and growth. It empowers you to lead with intention and authenticity, creating a meaningful impact on your team and organization.

By grounding your leadership in a clear philosophy, you set the stage for purposeful leadership that inspires others and fosters a positive organizational culture.

CRAFTING YOUR LEADERSHIP VISION

A leader without a vision is like a ship without a compass; both drift aimlessly, missing the destination.Crafting a leadership vision is the compass that guides a leader through uncharted waters; it provides direction, inspires others, and transforms challenges into opportunities. Without it, even the most capable leader may find themselves adrift, unable to reach their true potential or inspire their team.

Crafting your leadership vision is a vital step on the path to purposeful leadership. It begins with self-reflection, where you explore your values, passions, and the impact you wish to have on others. This introspection helps you identify what drives you and the legacy you want to create.

Articulating a clear vision is essential. It should be inspiring and provide direction, serving as a beacon that guides your decisions and actions. A compelling vision resonates not only with you but also with those you lead, fostering a sense of shared purpose and commitment.

Engaging with your team is crucial in this process. Collaborate with them to understand their aspirations and insights, which can enrich your vision and create a collective sense of ownership. This inclusivity strengthens relationships and encourages a supportive environment where everyone feels valued and motivated.

As you develop your vision, consider the broader context in which you operate. Reflect on the challenges and opportunities within your organization and industry. A purposeful leadership vision should be adaptable, allowing for adjustments as circumstances change while remaining true to your core values.

Communicating your vision effectively is another key aspect. Use storytelling to illustrate your vision and its significance, making it relatable and memorable. This approach can inspire action and encourage others to contribute to the realization of the vision.

Remain committed to your vision through consistent action. Align your decisions and behaviors with the vision you've crafted, demonstrating integrity and authenticity. As you navigate the journey of leadership, embrace feedback and continuously refine your vision, ensuring it remains relevant and impactful.

This commitment to purpose-driven leadership will empower you and those around you, fostering growth and success.

ALIGNING VALUES WITH PURPOSE

True fulfillment comes when values and purpose walk hand in hand. When your values and purpose align, every step you take leads to a meaningful journey.

Aligning values with purpose is essential for personal fulfillment and effective leadership. Values represent the core beliefs and principles that guide behavior and decision-making, reflecting what is truly important to individuals or organizations. In contrast, purpose embodies the overarching reason for existence, providing direction and motivation rooted in a desire to make a difference or achieve specific goals.

When individuals and organizations ensure that their actions reflect their core values, they create a cohesive framework that fosters authenticity and resilience.

This alignment leads to increased motivation, as a clear sense of purpose that resonates with personal or organizational values inspires greater engagement. Alignment serves as a compass, aiding consistent and principled decision-making even in challenging situations.

The benefits of aligning values with purpose are significant. Individuals often report higher levels of satisfaction and fulfillment when their actions mirror their core beliefs. Furthermore, a strong alignment helps navigate challenges effectively, as individuals and organizations remain grounded in their values.

In organizational settings, shared values and a collective sense of purpose can enhance teamwork and collaboration, fostering a sense of community.

Achieving alignment begins with self-reflection, where individuals engage in introspection to identify their personal values and articulate a clear purpose. Defining and communicating these values is crucial, as it ensures they guide actions consistently.

Setting goals that align with these values and purpose is also important, as it keeps daily actions reflective of this alignment. Regular evaluation allows for periodic assessment of whether actions truly align with stated values and purpose, enabling adjustments when necessary.

However, there are challenges to achieving this alignment. External pressures, such as societal expectations or organizational demands, can challenge personal values, leading to potential misalignment. The fear of conflict may prevent individuals from expressing their values or purpose, resulting in inauthentic behavior.

Aligning values with purpose is a dynamic and ongoing process that requires self-awareness, courage, and commitment. When achieved, this alignment enhances personal and professional fulfillment while positively impacting relationships and the broader community.

By fostering this alignment, individuals and organizations can navigate life's complexities with integrity and clarity.

THE ROLE OF SELF-AWARENESS

self-awareness stands as one of the foundational pillars for any leader aiming to lead with intentionality and impact. Self-awareness is the ability to consciously understand one's emotions, motivations, strengths, and weaknesses.

It helps leaders not only navigate their internal world but also build stronger relationships with others by promoting empathy, authenticity, and adaptability.

At the core of purposeful leadership lies the alignment between a leader's values and their actions. This alignment is only possible through deep self-awareness, as it allows leaders to reflect on their guiding principles and make deliberate choices that resonate with their mission.

When leaders are aware of their personal biases and emotional triggers, they are less likely to be swayed by external pressures and more capable of making decisions rooted in purpose rather than reaction.

Self-awareness fosters emotional intelligence, which is critical in managing teams effectively. Purposeful leaders who are attuned to their own emotions can better understand the emotional dynamics of their teams, creating environments where trust and psychological safety thrive.

This in turn enables team members to engage more fully, contribute creatively, and align their personal goals with the organization's vision.

Self-awareness also encourages humility in leadership. Purposeful leaders understand that leadership is not about perfection but about continuous learning and growth.

By recognizing their own limitations, they can seek out diverse perspectives, ask for feedback, and cultivate a culture of collaboration.

The journey toward self-awareness is an ongoing practice, not a one-time achievement. Leaders who dedicate themselves to regularly reflecting on their actions, seeking feedback, and understanding how their leadership impacts others, can evolve into more intentional, effective, and visionary guides for their teams and organizations.

Thus, self-awareness is the gateway through which purposeful leaders find clarity in their leadership and inspire others to follow their example.

THE IMPORTANCE OF EMOTIONAL INTELLIGENCE

Emotional intelligence lights the path to purposeful leadership; it transforms understanding into action and empathy into influence.Emotional intelligence is the compass for purposeful leadership; it enables leaders to navigate challenges with empathy, build authentic connections, and inspire trust.

In a world driven by results, it's the ability to understand emotions—both theirs and others—that transforms vision into reality, fostering a culture of collaboration and resilience. A leader's true strength lies not in authority, but in the power to connect, communicate, and cultivate a shared purpose.

Emotional intelligence (EI) is a critical component of effective leadership, especially for those pursuing a path of purposeful leadership. Emotional intelligence fundamentally starts with self-awareness, or the capacity to identify and comprehend one's own feelings.

Purposeful leaders who are self-aware can identify their strengths and weaknesses, fostering authenticity in their leadership style. This self-awareness nurtures both confidence and humility, essential traits for inspiring and guiding others.

Self-regulation is another vital aspect of emotional intelligence. Effective leaders with high EI can manage their emotions and reactions, allowing them to remain calm under pressure, make thoughtful decisions, and respond to challenges constructively. This ability not only sets a positive example for team members but also creates a more stable and supportive work environment.

Building solid relationships within a team requires empathy. Purposeful leaders who demonstrate empathy connect with their team members on a deeper level, fostering trust and loyalty. This connection encourages open communication and collaboration, which in turn enhances morale and productivity.

Strong social skills are essential for effective leadership. Leaders with high emotional intelligence navigate social complexities, build networks, and manage conflict with grace. These skills enhance team dynamics, enabling leaders to facilitate collaboration and create a cohesive work environment.

Leaders with emotional Intelligence are often intrinsically motivated and can inspire motivation in others. They possess a clear vision and purpose, which helps them rally their team around common goals. This shared motivation drives performance and engagement, aligning individual aspirations with organizational objectives.

Emotional intelligence contributes to better decision-making. Leaders who understand their emotions and those of their team can weigh the emotional impact of their decisions, leading to more thoughtful and inclusive outcomes. This approach enhances the decision-making process and increases team buy-in and commitment.

Being flexible is essential in the quickly evolving corporate environment of today. Leaders with high emotional intelligence are flexible and open to change. They can navigate uncertainty and inspire their teams to embrace change rather than resist it, fostering a culture of resilience.

Emotional intelligence is fundamental for purposeful leadership. It enhances self-awareness, self-regulation, empathy, social skills, motivation, decision-making, and adaptability.

Leaders who cultivate emotional intelligence not only improve their effectiveness but also create environments where their teams can thrive, ultimately driving success for the organization. As leaders embark on their journeys, honing their emotional intelligence enables them to lead with purpose, empathy, and impact.

TOOLS FOR SELF-REFLECTION AND ASSESSMENT

Self-reflection and assessment are essential tools for purposeful leadership, allowing leaders to gain insights into their strengths, weaknesses, values, and overall impact on others. Journaling is a powerful practice that enables leaders to process their thoughts and experiences.

By maintaining a daily or weekly journal, leaders can document challenges faced, decisions made, and lessons learned.

Gathering 360-degree feedback is another effective approach. This method involves soliciting input from peers, subordinates, and supervisors to obtain a comprehensive view of leadership effectiveness. Anonymous surveys can be particularly useful in assessing skills, behaviors, and the overall impact on team dynamics.

Conducting a personal SWOT analysis can also be beneficial. This involves identifying strengths, weaknesses, opportunities, and threats, allowing leaders to understand their current position and areas for growth. Leaders can create a grid to list personal attributes alongside external opportunities and potential obstacles.

Incorporating mindfulness and meditation into daily routines enhances self-awareness and emotional regulation. Mindfulness exercises, focused on breathing and present-moment awareness, can significantly improve a leader's ability to manage stress and make thoughtful decisions.

Coaching and mentoring provide valuable external perspectives and guidance. Regular sessions with a coach or mentor can help leaders discuss their goals, challenges, and progress in developing leadership skills.

Setting clear, measurable goals is crucial for accountability and direction in leadership development. Using the SMART framework

(Specific, Measurable, Achievable, Relevant, Time-bound) to define and regularly review goals ensures that leaders remain focused on their growth.

Engaging with specific reflection questions can stimulate deeper insights. Questions such as "What are my core values as a leader?" and "How do my decisions align with those values?" can prompt meaningful self-exploration.

Understanding personal values is vital for aligning actions with principles. Tools like value card sorts or online assessments can help leaders identify and prioritize their core values.

Various self-assessment tools are available to provide insights into leadership styles and competencies. Assessments like the Myers-Briggs Type Indicator (MBTI) or the Leadership Practices Inventory (LPI) can guide leaders in understanding their unique approaches.

Creating peer reflection groups fosters shared learning and accountability. Regular meetings with peers allow leaders to share experiences, challenges, and strategies for improvement.

By integrating these tools for self-reflection and assessment, leaders can cultivate greater self-awareness and adapt their leadership styles to better meet their teams' needs. Continuous reflection and evaluation are vital for personal and professional growth, enabling leaders to navigate their journeys with intention and clarity.

CULTIVATING A GROWTH MINDSET

Purposeful leadership is not found in reaching the summit, but in the journey of constant growth—where failures become lessons, challenges shape character, and the potential in others is cultivated into lasting impact. True leadership blossoms where growth meets purpose, and every challenge is a seed for both.

Cultivating a growth mindset is fundamental to purposeful leadership, as it allows leaders to approach their journey with a mindset of continuous learning, adaptability, and self-awareness. Leaders with a growth mindset view challenges as opportunities for growth rather than as obstacles.

They understand that difficulties and setbacks are a natural part of the leadership journey, and they embrace these challenges with the belief that they will emerge stronger and more capable. This resilience helps them maintain their sense of purpose even in uncertain or turbulent times.

A key aspect of the growth mindset in leadership is the ability to learn from failure. Purposeful leaders recognize that failure is not an endpoint but a critical part of the learning process. Instead of allowing mistakes to derail their progress, they reflect on what went wrong, extract valuable lessons, and adjust their strategies.

This perspective encourages innovation, as leaders are willing to take calculated risks knowing that any missteps will ultimately lead to deeper understanding and better solutions.

Purposeful leaders with a growth mindset also create a culture of feedback within their organizations. They encourage their teams to share insights and ideas openly, understanding that diverse perspectives contribute to better decision-making.

Feedback becomes a tool for continuous improvement, both for the leader and their team. This open dialogue fosters trust, transparency, and collaboration, which are essential components of a purpose-driven leadership approach.

In their own personal development, leaders with a growth mindset are lifelong learners. They seek out opportunities to acquire new skills, engage in self-reflection, and remain curious about the evolving world around them.

This commitment to personal growth keeps them agile and better equipped to adapt to changing circumstances. It also reinforces their sense of purpose, as they are continually aligning their actions and decisions with their deeper values and long-term goals.

At the core of purposeful leadership is the ability to uplift and empower others. Leaders with a growth mindset recognize the potential in their team members and actively work to nurture that potential. They act as coaches and mentors, offering direction and chances for development.

By investing in the development of those around them, they foster a culture of shared success, where each person's growth contributes to the collective advancement of the organization's purpose.

Cultivating a growth mindset on the path to purposeful leadership involves embracing the process of continual improvement. It requires a commitment to learning, an openness to feedback, and a willingness to face challenges with resilience and optimism.

Leaders who embody this mindset inspire others to grow alongside them, creating a powerful, purpose-driven culture that thrives on innovation, collaboration, and shared growth.

EMBRACING CHALLENGES AND LEARNING OPPORTUNITIES

True leadership is not found in ease, but in the courage to embrace challenges as stepping stones to purpose. It is through adversity that a leader's vision sharpens, resilience deepens, and values are tested.

In facing difficulties with an open heart and a steady mind, leaders transform obstacles into opportunities, failures into wisdom, and setbacks into stepping stones toward growth. Purposeful leadership is not the absence of struggle but the mastery of learning and evolving through it.

Embracing challenges and learning opportunities is a crucial part of the journey to purposeful leadership. Purposeful leaders are those who navigate with intention, guided by strong values and a clear vision.

Along the path, challenges are inevitable, but they are also the experiences that shape the most authentic and effective leaders. Instead of viewing obstacles as setbacks, these leaders see them as opportunities for growth, self-reflection, and innovation.

One of the key benefits of embracing challenges is the development of resilience. Leadership is not without adversity, and the ability to remain steadfast in difficult times is essential.

Each challenge builds a leader's capacity to withstand pressure, and with every setback, they learn to maintain composure. Resilient leaders inspire their teams, showing them that perseverance is key to long-term success.

Any leadership path inevitably involves failure. Purposeful leaders understand that failure is not a reflection of their worth but a necessary stepping stone to growth.

By embracing failure, they learn valuable lessons that help them refine their skills, make better decisions, and lead with greater wisdom. This growth mindset—where challenges are seen as learning opportunities—ensures that purposeful leaders continuously evolve.

Challenges also offer a space for innovation. Rather than sticking to conventional solutions, leaders who embrace difficulties are more willing to think creatively and explore new approaches.

This openness to change fosters innovation and positions leaders to adapt to the ever-evolving demands of their industries or teams. They become flexible problem-solvers, unafraid to explore uncharted territory.

Another important aspect of embracing challenges is the opportunity for personal growth and self-awareness. Difficult situations often reveal a leader's blind spots, weaknesses, and strengths.

By reflecting on how they react to challenges, leaders gain a deeper understanding of themselves, which allows them to make conscious improvements. Purposeful leaders use these insights to cultivate their leadership style, enhancing their effectiveness and empathy.

Facing challenges with empathy also strengthens relationships. When leaders confront obstacles, they gain an understanding of what their teams experience under pressure.

This shared experience can build stronger connections between leaders and their teams, fostering an environment of trust and support. Empathetic leadership creates a culture where individuals feel valued, heard, and motivated to give their best.

In moments of difficulty, leaders are often forced to reconnect with their core values and purpose. These situations test their ethical boundaries and commitment to their vision.

Purposeful leaders see challenges as opportunities to realign with their principles, making decisions that reflect their integrity. These moments of reflection ensure that leaders remain grounded and true to their mission, even in the face of adversity.

Leaders who embrace challenges are modeling a growth mindset for their teams. By demonstrating that challenges are not to be feared but welcomed, they encourage those around them to adopt the same perspective. This cultivates a culture of continuous learning and improvement within the organization, where everyone is open to growth and development.

Transparency is another hallmark of purposeful leadership in challenging times. When leaders face adversity, being open about the difficulties and involving their teams in finding solutions builds trust.

A transparent approach fosters a sense of accountability and inclusion, as everyone feels part of the process. This strengthens the bond between leaders and their teams, creating an environment where trust is a fundamental value.

The journey to purposeful leadership is defined by how a leader responds to challenges. It is through these moments of adversity that they develop the resilience, creativity, and self-awareness necessary to lead with authenticity. Embracing challenges not only strengthens the leader but also empowers those around them, creating a lasting impact on their organization and beyond.

STRATEGIES FOR CONTINUOUS PERSONAL DEVELOPMENT

Continuous personal development on the path to purposeful leadership requires intentional strategies and a commitment to growth. One of the key elements is self-reflection and self-awareness.

By regularly assessing personal values, strengths, and emotional intelligence, leaders can better understand their impact on others. Engaging in practices like journaling and seeking feedback from peers or mentors deepens this self-awareness and enhances leadership effectiveness.

Developing a growth mindset is essential, as it encourages leaders to view challenges as opportunities for growth rather than obstacles. Leaders who adopt this mindset are more resilient and adaptive, seeing failure as a chance to learn.

This attitude also fosters a culture of innovation and learning within their teams, encouraging continuous improvement and curiosity.

Lifelong learning is another cornerstone of leadership development. Staying informed about new ideas, trends, and skills is critical for making informed decisions and remaining effective in a leadership role.

This can be achieved through books, courses, seminars, and engaging with mentors. By continuously broadening their knowledge, leaders can better navigate the complexities of their roles and inspire those they lead.

Emotional intelligence, or EQ, plays a vital role in leadership. Leaders with high EQ are skilled in managing relationships, resolving conflicts, and leading with empathy.

Emotional intelligence can be developed through active listening, conflict resolution training, and being mindful of one's own and others' emotions. This helps create a supportive and productive work environment.

Setting clear, actionable goals is also important. Leaders benefit from setting SMART (Specific, Measurable, Achievable, Relevant, and Time-bound) goals that align with their personal and leadership development. Tracking progress using tools like habit trackers or regular reviews allows for continuous improvement and the ability to adjust strategies as needed.

Mentorship and peer learning are invaluable for leadership growth. By connecting with mentors, leaders gain access to wisdom and guidance that can shape their personal and professional journey. Engaging in peer learning groups, such as mastermind circles, offers collaborative problem-solving, accountability, and the exchange of new ideas.

Adaptability is crucial for leadership in today's rapidly changing world. Purposeful leaders must be prepared to embrace change and lead their teams through transitions. Staying open to new ideas and developing strong change management strategies helps leaders remain flexible and future-focused, ensuring long-term success.

Incorporating inclusivity and diversity into leadership practices enriches decision-making and team dynamics. Leaders who foster a culture of inclusion promote innovation and ensure that diverse perspectives are valued. This can be achieved through continuous learning on diversity issues and leading initiatives that promote equity within organizations.

Maintaining a healthy balance between personal well-being and work is essential for sustainable leadership. Burnout can limit growth, so it's important to prioritize self-care and encourage a culture of well-being within the team.

Practicing mindfulness, setting boundaries, and promoting work-life balance initiatives contribute to a healthier, more effective leadership style.

Visionary thinking is another critical aspect of purposeful leadership. By focusing on long-term goals and anticipating future trends, leaders can inspire their teams to work toward a shared vision.

Strategic foresight and the ability to influence others towards meaningful change are key attributes of a visionary leader, ensuring that their leadership has lasting, positive impact.

Through consistent self-awareness, a commitment to learning, and fostering an inclusive, resilient mindset, purposeful leaders can continuously grow and inspire those they lead.

CHAPTER

2

BUILDING HIGH-PERFORMING TEAMS

Leadership isn't about the destination, but about the journey shared. When trust fuels the team and purpose lights the way, excellence becomes inevitable and impact lasts beyond the moment. Lead with purpose, build with trust, and watch your team transform performance into legacy.

Building high-performing teams on the path to purposeful leadership requires a clear vision that resonates with the team's values and a strong foundation of trust and collaboration.

Purposeful leadership centers on guiding a team toward a meaningful goal that not only serves business objectives but also aligns with individual motivations and aspirations.

The journey begins with fostering a culture of open communication, where team members feel comfortable sharing their ideas and challenges. Encouraging diverse perspectives enriches decision-making, and it is essential for the leader to actively listen and demonstrate empathy. This helps create a sense of belonging and ensures that each member feels valued for their contributions.

A key aspect of building a high-performing team is establishing shared accountability. While each individual brings their own strengths, it is the collective responsibility that drives performance.

Leaders must set clear expectations and consistently support the team in achieving them, while also empowering individuals to take ownership of their roles. Purposeful leadership calls for recognizing the balance between providing direction and allowing space for autonomy, enabling the team to learn and grow from their experiences.

Trust plays a central role in this process. Respect for one another, consistency, and openness are the foundations of it. Leaders who demonstrate integrity in their actions and decisions create an environment where team members can rely on one another.

This trust leads to greater collaboration and a willingness to tackle challenges head-on, as the team knows they can depend on each other to succeed.

High-performing teams thrive under leaders who are not just focused on the end result but are also committed to nurturing personal growth and development. Purposeful leadership is about inspiring a shared vision that motivates the team to strive for excellence, while also cultivating an environment where individuals can pursue their potential and contribute meaningfully to the larger mission.

This holistic approach fosters resilience, innovation, and long-term success, as each team member feels connected to a purpose that goes beyond immediate tasks and goals.

CREATING A CULTURE OF TRUST AND COLLABORATION

Trust and collaboration are the roots of purposeful leadership; where they thrive, unity blossoms and visions come to life. In the garden of leadership, trust and collaboration are the seeds; nurture them well, and watch your vision blossom into reality.

Purposeful leadership is like a symphony; trust and collaboration are the harmony that turns individual notes into a powerful melody. When trust is the foundation, collaboration builds the walls; together, they create a fortress of purposeful leadership.

In the tapestry of leadership, trust weaves the threads of collaboration, creating a masterpiece of shared vision and purpose. A leader's true power lies not in command, but in the trust and collaboration that empower others to rise together.

In the realm of purposeful leadership, trust is the compass, and collaboration is the map; together, they guide the way to collective success. When trust lights the path, collaboration fuels the journey; purposeful leadership transforms obstacles into opportunities.

Creating a culture of trust and collaboration is essential for purposeful leadership. A leader with a clear purpose understands that their effectiveness hinges not only on their vision but also on their ability to unite people toward shared goals.

Trust begins with transparency; leaders must foster an environment where open communication flows freely in all directions—top-down, bottom-up, and laterally.

This openness helps reduce misunderstandings and ensures that everyone feels informed and valued. Sharing successes and challenges encourages a sense of ownership and accountability throughout the team.

Emotional intelligence and empathy are essential for developing solid connections. Purposeful leaders prioritize understanding the needs, motivations, and concerns of their team members. When individuals feel understood and respected, they are more likely to collaborate and trust their leader. Demonstrating emotional intelligence involves active listening, compassion, and thoughtful responses to feedback.

Empowerment is another crucial aspect of cultivating a culture of trust and collaboration. Leaders should entrust team members with responsibility, fostering engagement and motivation.

By giving individuals the autonomy to make decisions and contribute meaningfully, leaders not only enhance collaboration but also encourage ownership of their roles within the broader mission. This approach transforms the dynamic from one of control to one of partnership.

Modeling integrity and authenticity further strengthens trust. Leaders who align their words with their actions set a powerful example for their teams. Purposeful leaders embrace vulnerability, admitting mistakes and inviting others to learn from them. This openness reinforces a culture of growth, allowing team members to feel safe in taking risks and exploring new ideas.

Creating a psychologically safe environment is essential for nurturing collaboration. Team members must feel comfortable sharing their ideas without fear of judgment.

A culture of trust thrives when individuals are encouraged to challenge ideas, propose solutions, and contribute openly. Purposeful leaders celebrate diversity of thought and ensure that all voices are heard, reinforcing inclusivity.

Recognizing and celebrating contributions also plays a significant role in fostering trust. Purposeful leaders understand that acknowledgment and recognition boost morale and strengthen bonds within the team.

By celebrating both individual and collective achievements, leaders affirm that every effort is valued, creating a sense of belonging and shared purpose.

Investing in the development of team members through mentorship and coaching is another hallmark of purposeful leadership. By nurturing the growth of others, leaders strengthen trust and demonstrate a commitment to their long-term success.

This investment not only deepens collaboration but also ensures the sustainability of leadership within the organization.

Purposeful leadership transcends mere direction; it involves cultivating a culture of trust and collaboration that empowers everyone to work together toward a meaningful vision.

By embracing transparency, empathy, empowerment, integrity, and inclusion, purposeful leaders foster high-performing teams that are deeply connected to the mission and to one another. This culture of trust and collaboration becomes the foundation for lasting impact and sustainable leadership.

THE ELEMENTS OF TRUST IN TEAMS

Trust is the foundation upon which great teams are built; it transforms individual potential into collective strength. In an environment where reliability, vulnerability, and open communication thrive, innovation blossoms, and purpose ignites.

When trust flows freely, accountability nurtures growth, allowing teams to rise together, overcoming challenges and achieving greatness as one.Trust is the glue that binds teams; without it, collaboration crumbles, but with it, purpose flourishes.

Trust is a cornerstone of effective teamwork and purposeful leadership. In a team setting, trust fosters collaboration and open communication, enabling members to feel safe in sharing ideas and taking risks. When team members trust each other, they are more likely to engage in honest discussions, provide constructive feedback, and support one another through challenges.

One essential element of trust is reliability. Team members must consistently deliver on their commitments and uphold their responsibilities. When individuals demonstrate reliability, it reinforces the belief that everyone can depend on one another, creating a sense of security within the team.

Another critical aspect is vulnerability. Purposeful leaders encourage vulnerability by modeling openness and sharing their own challenges. This creates an environment where team members feel comfortable expressing their fears and uncertainties, leading to deeper connections and mutual support. When vulnerability is embraced, it cultivates a culture of empathy and understanding, further solidifying trust.

Effective communication also plays a vital role in building trust. Clear and transparent communication helps prevent misunderstandings and fosters an atmosphere of respect. Team members should feel free to voice their opinions and concerns without fear of judgment, knowing their contributions are valued.

Inclusivity is another key element. Teams that prioritize inclusivity create a sense of belonging, where all voices are heard and respected. Purposeful leaders actively seek diverse perspectives, recognizing that varied viewpoints enhance problem-solving and innovation. This inclusivity strengthens trust among team members, as everyone feels they are an integral part of the team's success.

Accountability is crucial in establishing trust. When team members hold themselves and each other accountable for their actions, it reinforces a culture of integrity. Leaders should encourage a mindset where mistakes are viewed as learning opportunities rather than failures, promoting a growth-oriented approach.

By weaving these elements of trust into the fabric of teamwork, leaders pave the way for a more engaged, motivated, and high-performing team. This trust not only drives individual performance but also aligns the team towards a common purpose, ultimately leading to collective success.

TECHNIQUES FOR FOSTERING COLLABORATION

Collaboration blooms where trust is sown and purpose is shared; together, we cultivate a garden of innovation and success, where every voice nurtures the vision and every effort grows the dream.

Fostering collaboration is essential on the path to purposeful leadership. One effective technique is to cultivate an open communication environment where team members feel comfortable sharing their ideas and feedback. Encouraging regular check-ins and team meetings can facilitate this, allowing for a free flow of thoughts and concerns.

Developing trust among team members is another essential component. Leaders can achieve this by being transparent about their own challenges and decisions, demonstrating vulnerability and authenticity. When team members see their leader as relatable, they are more likely to contribute openly and honestly.

Promoting shared goals can unify the team, directing collective efforts toward a common purpose. Leaders should articulate the vision clearly and ensure that every team member understands their role in achieving that vision. This shared understanding enhances collaboration as individuals see how their contributions impact the larger objectives.

Creating opportunities for cross-functional collaboration also enhances teamwork. By encouraging collaboration between different departments or specialties, leaders can foster diverse perspectives and innovative solutions. Organizing workshops or team-building activities that involve various skill sets can help break down silos and strengthen relationships.

Acknowledging and commemorating cooperative endeavors can strengthen the significance of teamwork. Acknowledging individual and team achievements fosters a culture of appreciation and motivates members to continue working together effectively.

Providing access to collaborative tools and technology can streamline the process. Utilizing platforms that facilitate communication, project management, and document sharing can significantly enhance collaboration efforts. Leaders should ensure that their teams have the resources they need to collaborate efficiently and effectively.

By implementing these techniques, leaders can create a collaborative environment that empowers individuals and drives collective success on the path to purposeful leadership.

EFFECTIVE COMMUNICATION STRATEGIES

Effective communication is the bridge that transforms purpose into action, allowing leaders to illuminate paths and inspire collaboration. When words resonate with clarity and empathy, they weave a tapestry of trust that empowers teams to turn vision into reality.

Effective communication is a cornerstone of purposeful leadership, essential for fostering meaningful connections and driving team success.

One key strategy is active listening, which involves engaging fully with the speaker and demonstrating genuine interest in their perspective. This builds trust and encourages open dialogue, enabling leaders to understand their team members better.

Clarity and conciseness are equally important in communication. Leaders should convey messages clearly and succinctly, avoiding jargon and unnecessary complexity. This approach reduces misunderstandings and ensures that everyone is aligned, facilitating effective decision-making.

Empathy plays a critical role in communication, allowing leaders to recognize and validate the feelings and emotions of others. By fostering a supportive environment, leaders encourage team members to express their thoughts and concerns, enhancing morale and collaboration.

Non-verbal communication also deserves attention. Leaders must be aware of body language, facial expressions, and tone of voice, as these non-verbal cues can reinforce or contradict verbal messages, strengthening overall communication effectiveness.

Establishing feedback mechanisms is vital for a culture of continuous improvement. Leaders should create regular channels for giving and receiving feedback, allowing them to adapt their strategies based on team input and ensuring everyone feels valued.

Adaptability in communication styles is essential, as leaders must tailor their approaches to suit different audiences and contexts. This adaptability helps leaders connect with diverse teams and stakeholders, making messages more relatable and effective.

Encouraging open dialogue creates a safe space for team members to share ideas and concerns without fear of repercussions. This practice promotes innovation and problem-solving, as team members feel empowered to contribute.

Another crucial aspect of effective communication is vision sharing. Leaders should clearly articulate the organization's vision, goals, and values to align the team's efforts and foster a sense of purpose, motivating individuals to work toward common objectives.

When conflicts arise, addressing them directly and constructively is important. Leaders should facilitate discussions to reach mutually beneficial solutions, preventing escalation and promoting collaboration, which strengthens team cohesion.

When used effectively, storytelling can be a leader's greatest communication weapon. Using narratives to convey messages can make complex ideas relatable, enhancing engagement and fostering emotional connections among team members.

By implementing these strategies, leaders cultivate a culture of effective communication, essential for driving engagement, fostering collaboration, and achieving organizational goals. Purposeful leadership thrives on clarity, connection, and commitment, all amplified through effective communication.

THE ART OF ACTIVE LISTENING

To lead with purpose, listen with intent; for in the echoes of others, true wisdom is spent. Effective leadership is rooted in listening; the more we hear, the farther we can lead. Leadership flourishes in the soil of active listening; by embracing the voices around us, we cultivate understanding, trust, and a shared vision that guides us all forward.

The art of active listening is a crucial skill for anyone aspiring to be a purposeful leader. It involves more than just hearing words; it requires genuine engagement with the speaker. Active listening fosters deeper connections and promotes trust, as it demonstrates respect for others' perspectives and experiences.

In the context of leadership, active listening allows leaders to understand their team members better, acknowledging their thoughts and feelings.

This understanding creates an environment where individuals feel valued and empowered, enhancing collaboration and innovation. Leaders who practice active listening are often more effective in resolving conflicts, as they can navigate disagreements with empathy and insight.

Moreover, active listening cultivates a culture of open communication. By modeling this behavior, leaders encourage their teams to share ideas and feedback freely, which can lead to improved decision-making and problem-solving.

It also helps leaders to glean important insights from diverse viewpoints, enriching their understanding of challenges and opportunities.

In the pursuit of purposeful leadership, embracing active listening can transform interactions. It shifts the focus from merely directing others to genuinely connecting with them.

This connection lays the foundation for inspiring and motivating teams, guiding them toward shared goals and a unified vision. Ultimately, the art of active listening empowers leaders to create a more inclusive, effective, and engaged workplace.

DELIVERING FEEDBACK WITH IMPACT

True wisdom in leadership lies in recognizing that feedback is a gift—a mirror reflecting not only the journey of improvement but also the boundless potential within each individual.

By cultivating a culture of open dialogue and support, leaders transform feedback into a powerful force that ignites passion, fosters resilience, and paves the way for extraordinary achievements.Great leaders understand that feedback is not just a critique; it is a seed planted in the soil of potential, nurturing growth and illuminating the path to success.

True leadership is measured not by the feedback given, but by the growth it inspires.Effective leadership is not merely about issuing feedback; it lies in nurturing growth through every conversation, turning insights into actions that empower individuals and strengthen the team. In this way, every piece of feedback becomes a stepping stone on the path to collective success.

Delivering feedback with impact is a vital component of purposeful leadership. It requires not just the ability to communicate effectively, but also the intention to foster growth and development in individuals and teams.

Purposeful leaders understand that feedback is a tool for learning, not just evaluation.

To deliver impactful feedback, leaders must create an environment of trust and psychological safety. When team members feel safe, they are more likely to engage openly with the feedback process. This environment encourages honest discussions, where individuals can reflect on their performance without fear of repercussions.

Leaders should approach feedback as a dialogue, inviting input and fostering a two-way conversation that empowers employees to take ownership of their growth.

Clarity is essential when providing feedback. Leaders should aim to be specific, highlighting particular behaviors or outcomes rather than making generalized statements. This specificity helps recipients understand exactly what they did well or where they can improve, allowing them to take actionable steps.

Balancing constructive criticism with positive reinforcement ensures that feedback remains motivating rather than demoralizing. Recognizing achievements alongside areas for improvement helps individuals see the full picture of their performance and maintains their engagement.

Another important factor in feedback efficacy is timing. Offering feedback soon after an event or behavior allows for a more relevant discussion, reinforcing learning while the experience is still fresh in mind.

Leaders should be attuned to the individual needs of their team members, adjusting their approach based on each person's unique circumstances and learning styles.

To enhance the impact of feedback, purposeful leaders should model the behavior they wish to see. Demonstrating openness to receiving feedback themselves shows that it is a reciprocal process. This sets a powerful example for team members, encouraging a culture of continuous improvement where feedback is valued and sought after.

Delivering feedback with impact is about more than just communicating information; it's about fostering growth, building relationships, and driving performance.

By prioritizing clarity, trust, and a genuine investment in their team's development, leaders can transform feedback into a powerful catalyst for purposeful leadership and organizational success.

EMPOWERING TEAM MEMBERS

Empowerment in leadership transcends mere authority; it is the art of nurturing potential within each team member. By fostering an environment of trust and open communication, leaders illuminate the path where every voice is valued, every idea has merit, and every contribution is a step toward a shared vision.

In this space, individuals transform from mere followers into passionate creators of their collective destiny, driven by purpose and united in the pursuit of excellence.

Empowering team members is a cornerstone of purposeful leadership, fostering an environment where individuals feel valued, engaged, and motivated. Purposeful leaders prioritize creating a culture of trust and collaboration, encouraging team members to take ownership of their roles.

This empowerment begins with open communication, where leaders actively listen to ideas and concerns, allowing team members to feel heard and respected.

By providing opportunities for professional development, leaders help team members acquire new skills and gain confidence in their abilities. This builds the team cohesively and improves individual performance as well.

Encouraging autonomy is another key aspect of empowerment. When team members are given the freedom to make decisions and explore innovative solutions, they develop a sense of responsibility and pride in their work.

Recognizing and celebrating achievements, both big and small, reinforces a sense of belonging and motivation. Purposeful leaders understand the importance of aligning team goals with the organization's vision, ensuring that each member sees how their contributions matter. This alignment fosters a deeper connection to the work and a shared commitment to achieving common objectives.

Empowering team members creates a dynamic where everyone thrives. Purposeful leadership is about nurturing potential, fostering collaboration, and building a resilient team that is equipped to tackle challenges with creativity and enthusiasm.

In this empowered environment, team members are not just followers; they become active contributors to the organization's success, driven by a shared purpose and a commitment to excellence.

DELEGATION AND EMPOWERMENT TECHNIQUES

True leadership lies not in holding power, but in empowering others; delegate with trust, communicate with clarity, and watch your team transform into a force of innovation and strength.Leadership is the art of enabling others to shine; when you delegate with intention and empower with confidence, you create a tapestry of collective strength.

In this shared journey, communication becomes the bridge that connects visions, while trust fosters an environment where creativity flourishes. Embrace the wisdom that the greatest leaders are not those who carry the weight alone, but those who inspire and uplift their teams, cultivating a legacy of collaboration and shared success.

Delegation and empowerment are vital techniques on the path to purposeful leadership, fostering a culture of trust and collaboration. Effective delegation involves assigning tasks and responsibilities to team members based on their strengths and capabilities.

By doing so, leaders not only lighten their own workload but also provide opportunities for others to develop skills and gain confidence.

Empowerment goes hand in hand with delegation. It involves granting individuals the authority to make decisions and take ownership of their tasks. This creates a sense of accountability and encourages innovation, as team members feel trusted to contribute their ideas and solutions.

Leaders can empower their teams by providing the necessary resources, training, and support, while also encouraging a growth mindset that embraces learning from mistakes.

Communication plays a critical role in both delegation and empowerment. Leaders must clearly articulate expectations, provide constructive feedback, and encourage open dialogue. This transparency fosters a supportive environment where team members feel comfortable sharing their thoughts and concerns.

Building relationships based on trust is essential for successful delegation and empowerment. Leaders who take the time to understand their team members' strengths, weaknesses, and aspirations can tailor their approach to maximize effectiveness. Acknowledging achievements and celebrating successes reinforces the value of contribution and motivates continued performance.

Leaders should cultivate a culture of collaboration, where team members are encouraged to work together and support one another. This collaborative mindset fosters a sense of belonging and camaraderie in addition to increasing productivity.

Delegation and empowerment techniques are crucial for purposeful leadership. By effectively assigning responsibilities, fostering a culture of trust, and promoting open communication, leaders can inspire their teams to reach their full potential, driving both individual growth and organizational success.

ENCOURAGING INITIATIVE AND INNOVATION

True leadership flourishes in an environment where initiative is nurtured; it is through the courage to innovate that we unlock the potential for profound change. Embrace the ideas of your team, celebrate the brave steps they take, and cultivate a culture where every voice matters.

In doing so, you not only inspire creativity but also empower those around you to transform vision into reality, forging a path toward a brighter and more purposeful future.

True leadership flourishes in an environment where initiative is nurtured, for it is through the courage to innovate that we unlock the potential for profound change.

Encouraging initiative and innovation is vital for purposeful leadership, as it fosters an environment where creativity and proactive thinking thrive. Leaders who promote initiative empower their teams to take ownership of their work and explore new ideas, enhancing engagement and motivation.

This autonomy encourages individuals to think critically and develop solutions to challenges rather than simply following established procedures.

Innovation flourishes when leaders cultivate a culture that values experimentation and embraces failure as a learning opportunity. By encouraging team members to share their ideas without fear of criticism, leaders create a safe space for brainstorming and collaboration.

This inclusivity not only enhances team dynamics but also brings diverse perspectives to the table, leading to more comprehensive and innovative solutions.

Leaders can model initiative by demonstrating a willingness to take calculated risks themselves. When team members see their leaders exploring new approaches and challenging the status quo, they are inspired to do the same. This leadership by example establishes a norm where taking initiative is celebrated and rewarded.

Fostering initiative also involves providing the necessary resources and support. Leaders should ensure that their teams have access to training, tools, and time for exploration.

This investment in development signals that the organization values innovation and is committed to supporting employees in their endeavors.

Recognizing and celebrating successful initiatives, no matter how small, reinforces the importance of innovation within the organization. Acknowledgement motivates others to contribute their ideas and reinforces the message that their input is valued.

Purposeful leadership thrives on a foundation of initiative and innovation. By creating a supportive environment, leading by example, and recognizing contributions, leaders can inspire their teams to embrace creativity and drive meaningful change.

This approach not only enhances organizational performance but also cultivates a culture of continuous improvement and adaptability, essential for navigating today's dynamic landscape.

CHAPTER

3

LEADING WITH PURPOSE AND IMPACT

Leadership is the art of guiding others with a vision anchored in purpose; it transforms not just the leader but also the lives of those they touch, igniting a ripple of impact that echoes far beyond their own reach. True leadership is not measured by the power you wield, but by the purpose you serve and the impact you inspire.

Leading with purpose and impact is at the heart of purposeful leadership. It begins with a clear understanding of one's values and vision, enabling leaders to align their actions and decisions with a greater mission. This alignment fosters authenticity, allowing leaders to inspire trust and motivate their teams.

Purposeful leadership transcends traditional metrics of success, focusing instead on meaningful outcomes that contribute to the well-being of individuals and communities. Leaders who prioritize purpose encourage collaboration and innovation, creating an environment where team members feel valued and empowered to share their ideas.

Impact is achieved when leaders actively engage with their teams, listen to diverse perspectives, and cultivate a culture of accountability. By demonstrating empathy and resilience, they model the behaviors that promote growth and adaptation in the face of challenges.

Leading with purpose means recognizing the broader implications of one's actions.

Purposeful leaders think beyond immediate results, considering the long-term effects of their decisions on stakeholders and the environment. This holistic approach not only drives sustainable success but also builds a legacy of positive change.

leading with purpose and impact requires a commitment to continuous learning and self-reflection. Leaders who embrace this journey are not only effective in their roles but also serve as catalysts for transformation, guiding their organizations toward a future that is both innovative and responsible.

ESTABLISHING A PURPOSE-DRIVEN CULTURE

Purpose-driven leadership is the beacon that illuminates the path to collective greatness; when each individual's passion is woven into the fabric of a shared mission, challenges become stepping stones, and dreams are forged into reality. In this synergy, organizations flourish, communities thrive, and the essence of leadership transcends mere authority, evolving into a transformative force that inspires action and ignites potential.

True leadership ignites a purpose-driven culture, where every individual's passion aligns with a shared mission, transforming challenges into opportunities and aspirations into achievements.

Establishing a purpose-driven culture is essential for organizations aiming to foster purposeful leadership. At the core of this approach lies a clear and compelling purpose that resonates with every member of the organization.

When employees understand and connect with the organization's purpose, they are more likely to be engaged, motivated, and aligned in their efforts.

Creating a purpose-driven culture begins with leadership. Leaders must embody the organization's purpose, demonstrating its importance through their actions and decisions.

This authenticity inspires others to embrace the purpose and align their personal values with the organization's mission. Regularly communicating the purpose reinforces its significance, ensuring that it remains front and center in daily operations and decision-making.

Encouraging open dialogue and feedback is crucial for nurturing a purpose-driven culture. By fostering an environment where employees feel safe to express their thoughts and ideas, organizations can cultivate a sense of belonging and ownership. This inclusivity not only strengthens commitment but also encourages innovation and collaboration as diverse perspectives contribute to a shared vision.

Recognition and reward systems also play a vital role in reinforcing a purpose-driven culture. Celebrating achievements that align with the organization's purpose motivates employees to strive for excellence and remain engaged. When individuals see their contributions making a meaningful impact, it deepens their connection to the organization and its goals.

Integrating the purpose into the organization's practices and policies ensures that it permeates every aspect of the business. From recruitment to performance evaluations, aligning these processes with the established purpose helps attract and retain individuals who resonate with the organization's mission.

This alignment fosters a cohesive workforce dedicated to achieving shared goals.

As organizations navigate challenges and changes, maintaining a purpose-driven culture can provide stability and direction. In times of uncertainty, a clear purpose serves as a guiding star, helping employees stay focused and resilient.

This commitment to purpose enhances overall organizational performance, as teams collaborate more effectively and make decisions that align with the collective mission.

establishing a purpose-driven culture is a powerful pathway to purposeful leadership. By embedding purpose into the organization's fabric, leaders can inspire engagement, foster collaboration, and navigate challenges with resilience, ultimately driving sustainable success.

DEFINING ORGANIZATIONAL PURPOSE

Leadership rooted in purpose not only charts a course for success but also ignites passion within individuals. When an organization's mission resonates deeply, it empowers each member to contribute meaningfully, turning challenges into opportunities and dreams into realities.

In the pursuit of a shared vision, leaders become catalysts for change, forging a legacy that inspires future generations. True leadership begins with a clear purpose; it transforms vision into action and inspires others to journey together toward a common mission.

Defining organizational purpose is a crucial step on the path to purposeful leadership, as it establishes a foundation upon which the entire organization can operate. Purpose serves as a guiding star, influencing decision-making, shaping culture, and driving employee engagement. It is not merely a statement but a reflection of the values and aspirations that define the organization.

A clear and compelling organizational purpose inspires individuals to connect their personal goals with the larger mission, fostering a sense of belonging and motivation.

When leaders articulate a purpose that resonates, it creates a shared understanding among team members, aligning their efforts towards common objectives. This alignment is essential for building trust and collaboration, which are vital for high-performing teams.

Moreover, a well-defined purpose can enhance resilience in the face of challenges. Organizations grounded in a strong purpose are better equipped to navigate uncertainty, as their teams are motivated by a deeper commitment to their mission rather than merely responding to external pressures. This perspective empowers leaders to make strategic decisions that reflect their values and long-term vision.

Purposeful leadership involves continuously revisiting and refining the organizational purpose, ensuring it remains relevant in a changing environment. Engaging stakeholders in this process fosters inclusivity and harnesses diverse perspectives, making the purpose more robust and representative of the entire organization.

Defining organizational purpose is not a one-time task but an ongoing journey that cultivates a culture of purposefulness. Leaders who prioritize this aspect of their organizations can inspire their teams, drive meaningful impact, and ultimately create a legacy that extends beyond the bottom line.

The journey toward purposeful leadership, therefore, begins with a commitment to understanding and articulating the true essence of the organization's mission and values.

ALIGNING TEAM GOALS WITH PURPOSE

True leadership aligns vision with purpose, turning individual goals into a shared mission that inspires growth, innovation, and lasting impact.

Purposeful leadership is the art of weaving personal aspirations into the fabric of a collective mission, where every goal serves a higher vision, and every step forward carries the weight of meaning. When leaders align purpose with action, they don't just lead teams;

they ignite movements that transcend individual success, fostering a legacy of growth, fulfillment, and transformative impact.

Aligning team goals with purpose on the path to purposeful leadership is about more than just setting targets; it's about fostering a deeper connection between the work being done and the larger mission behind it.

Purposeful leadership begins with a clear and compelling vision that resonates with both the organization and the individuals within it. When a team understands why their work matters beyond just meeting objectives, it creates a strong sense of meaning and motivation that drives performance and engagement.

This alignment process involves translating the broader purpose into actionable and specific goals. It's essential that these goals are not only clear but also directly tied to the overarching vision. When team members see how their contributions fit into the bigger picture, they are more invested in achieving success. Purpose-driven goals should be attainable and measurable, so progress is visible, keeping the team focused and on track.

In purposeful leadership, empowering the team to take ownership of their work is crucial. Autonomy allows individuals to take the initiative and find creative solutions to challenges. When leaders trust their teams to navigate toward the goals in their own way, it fosters a sense of responsibility and pride in the outcomes.

This level of ownership also deepens the connection to the purpose, as team members feel more personally accountable for contributing to something meaningful.

Regular alignment checks are a vital part of ensuring that the team remains connected to the purpose. Leaders who facilitate ongoing feedback and open communication help the team stay on course, continuously adjusting and refining goals as needed.

Purpose should not be a static statement but a living part of the team's daily efforts. By reflecting on progress and recalibrating when necessary, the team can maintain a strong alignment between their objectives and the larger mission.

Purposeful leadership also involves supporting the individual growth of each team member. A team is made up of people with their own personal aspirations, and aligning these personal goals with the team's purpose enhances both individual and collective success.

Leaders can provide opportunities for personal development that are in harmony with the team's broader objectives, ensuring that growth happens on both a personal and organizational level.

Celebrating achievements and reflecting on the impact of the team's work reinforces the alignment between goals and purpose. Recognizing milestones is an important way to maintain motivation and highlight the significance of the work being done.

It's not just about hitting targets but understanding how those achievements contribute to the greater good. Purposeful leaders remind their teams of the real-world impact of their efforts, keeping the purpose alive and central to the team's mission.

Aligning team goals with purpose on the path to purposeful leadership creates a culture of engagement, innovation, and fulfillment. Teams that are driven by a sense of purpose are more resilient, more creative, and more motivated to achieve lasting success.

Purposeful leadership is about guiding with intention, connecting the dots between individual effort and collective impact, and cultivating a shared sense of meaning that drives both personal and organizational growth.

MOTIVATING AND INSPIRING OTHERS

Purposeful leadership is not defined by the power to direct, but by the ability to inspire others to discover their own strength, align their passions with a greater mission, and grow into leaders themselves.

It is a journey of uplifting others, where success is measured not by what you achieve alone, but by the legacy of empowerment you leave behind.True leadership is not about commanding from above, but igniting a shared vision that empowers others to rise, grow, and lead with purpose.

Motivating and inspiring others on the path to purposeful leadership begins with leading by example. The most effective way to encourage others is through embodying the values, behaviors, and attitudes you wish to instill in your team. When people see a leader demonstrating commitment, integrity, and resilience, they naturally feel inspired to follow.

An important aspect of this is communicating a vision that is clear and passionate. When leaders articulate a compelling goal that resonates with their team, it gives people a sense of purpose. The enthusiasm and belief that a leader shows for this vision can ignite a shared passion, encouraging others to align their efforts toward that greater objective.

Equally crucial is the ability to empower those around you. Purposeful leadership involves helping others recognize and unleash their potential. By fostering a culture where everyone feels their voice matters, where ideas are encouraged, and autonomy is given, individuals gain confidence and motivation to step up and take responsibility.

Cultivating a growth mindset is another way leaders can inspire their teams. When challenges are framed as opportunities for development, people become more willing to take risks and learn from their mistakes. By creating an environment where experimentation is encouraged and failure is seen as part of the journey, a leader helps to nurture resilience and continuous improvement.

Providing meaningful feedback and recognition is also vital in maintaining motivation. People are driven by feeling appreciated for their work. When leaders take the time to celebrate achievements and offer constructive feedback, it fosters a sense of accomplishment and drives people to continue performing at their best.

Building strong relationships is at the heart of inspiring others. Purposeful leaders take the time to understand their team members' needs, strengths, and aspirations. By demonstrating empathy, listening actively, and offering genuine support, a leader can cultivate loyalty and trust, creating a bond that motivates individuals to invest in their work and the team's shared goals.

Creating a shared sense of purpose goes hand in hand with inspiring others. When leaders ensure that everyone understands how their contributions matter to the larger mission, it gives their work meaning beyond the immediate task at hand. This connection between individual effort and collective success provides a deep, intrinsic motivation that is far more enduring than external incentives.

In challenging times, the ability to remain resilient and positive is a powerful motivator for others. Leaders who demonstrate calm, adaptability, and optimism in the face of adversity inspire their teams to do the same. Resilience is contagious; when people see their leader stay focused and proactive, it encourages them to persevere and stay committed even in the face of obstacles.

Developing future leaders is also a key responsibility of purposeful leadership. By mentoring and investing in the growth of others, leaders not only motivate but also ensure that their values and vision endure through the next generation. A leader's legacy is defined by the leaders they help to develop, ensuring that the journey continues beyond their own tenure.

Purposeful leadership fosters collaboration. When leaders promote teamwork and encourage diverse perspectives, it creates a culture of innovation and unity. Collaboration brings people together, allows for shared ownership of successes, and fuels the motivation to work toward collective goals.

Motivating and inspiring others as a leader is not about exerting control or authority. It's about nurturing a shared passion, empowering individuals, and creating an environment where people feel supported and valued. Purposeful leadership is a journey of mutual growth and achievement, where both the leader and their team reach new heights together.

UNDERSTANDING INTRINSIC VS. EXTRINSIC MOTIVATION

True leadership is born from the fire within, not the accolades from without. When a leader's purpose is fueled by intrinsic passion, the journey becomes its own reward, and success follows as a byproduct of authenticity and unwavering vision. Extrinsic rewards may illuminate the path, but it is the inner flame that sustains the course.

Intrinsic and extrinsic motivation are key drivers on the path to purposeful leadership. Intrinsic motivation comes from within, fueled by personal satisfaction, a sense of achievement, or the fulfillment of a deep-seated passion.

When leaders are intrinsically motivated, they lead with a sense of purpose, driven by values and beliefs rather than external rewards. This inner drive creates a more authentic form of leadership, where actions are aligned with one's core purpose, resulting in greater engagement and resilience. Intrinsic motivation fosters a sense of ownership and commitment to personal growth and the well-being of the team or organization.

In contrast, extrinsic motivation is powered by external factors such as rewards, recognition, or avoiding negative consequences. Leaders motivated by extrinsic rewards often focus on achieving specific outcomes to gain approval, status, or material benefits.

While this can be effective in the short term, it may lack the deeper connection necessary for sustained purpose-driven leadership. A leader relying too much on extrinsic motivators may find it harder to navigate challenges when external rewards are not immediately apparent.

Purposeful leadership blends both intrinsic and extrinsic motivation. While intrinsic motivation drives a leader's inner commitment to vision and values, extrinsic factors such as recognition or success can help reinforce and encourage positive behaviors.

However, the key is maintaining a balance where external rewards complement rather than replace the internal drive to lead with purpose. Leaders who understand this dynamic can harness both motivations effectively, creating a leadership style that is not only impactful but also sustainable in the long run.

STRATEGIES FOR INSPIRING TEAM ENGAGEMENT

Engagement blooms in an environment of trust and purpose; when leaders inspire their teams to see the bigger picture, they unlock the potential for greatness within every individual. True leadership ignites engagement by weaving a tapestry of trust, purpose, and collaboration.

When leaders inspire their teams to embrace a shared vision, they not only unlock individual potential but also cultivate a collective strength that drives innovation and resilience. In this synergy, every voice matters, every contribution counts, and together, they forge a path to extraordinary achievement.

Inspiring team engagement is crucial for effective and purposeful leadership. One of the foundational elements is establishing a clear vision. Leaders should articulate a compelling purpose that aligns with the team's values and goals.

When team members understand how their contributions impact the larger objectives, they feel more connected and motivated. Setting specific, measurable, achievable, relevant, and time-bound (SMART) goals also helps individuals see how their roles fit into the broader mission.

Fostering open communication is equally essential. Encouraging feedback through various channels allows team members to share ideas and concerns without fear of repercussions. Leaders should practice active listening, demonstrating respect for diverse perspectives, which builds trust and cultivates a culture of openness.

Empowerment plays a significant role in engagement as well. By delegating responsibility, leaders allow individuals to take ownership of their work, instilling confidence and encouraging initiative. Supporting autonomy enables team members to make decisions and express creativity within their roles, further enhancing their sense of ownership and accountability.

Cultivating a positive culture is vital for maintaining high levels of engagement. Regularly recognizing contributions—both big and small—motivates team members and reinforces positive behavior. Promoting inclusivity, where diverse thoughts and experiences are valued, leads to greater collaboration and innovation.

Investing in development opportunities is another key aspect. Providing professional development and training programs helps team members grow their skills and advance their careers. Additionally, establishing mentorship programs can pair individuals with mentors who offer guidance and support, enhancing personal and professional growth.

Promoting teamwork among members cultivates a feeling of belonging. Organizing team-building activities strengthens relationships, while cross-functional projects promote knowledge sharing and broaden perspectives.

Leading by example is crucial in inspiring engagement. Leaders who demonstrate enthusiasm and commitment to the team's goals naturally encourage others to follow suit. Practicing transparency by being open about challenges and successes fosters trust and encourages team members to share their own experiences.

Promoting work-life balance also plays an important role in team engagement. Offering flexible work arrangements and encouraging breaks help team members manage their personal and professional lives effectively.

inspiring team engagement is an ongoing journey that requires purposeful leadership and a commitment to fostering a positive work environment.

By implementing these strategies, leaders can cultivate motivated, collaborative, and high-performing teams aligned with the organization's mission and vision. Engaged teams not only achieve better results but also contribute to a more vibrant and fulfilling workplace culture.

NAVIGATING CHANGE AND CHALLENGES

Adversity and change serve as a furnace for the development of true leadership. It is the ability to remain anchored in purpose while adapting with grace and strength to every challenge. It is the wisdom to see change not as a disruption, but as a call to evolve, to lead with empathy and vision, and to inspire others to rise above uncertainty.

Purposeful leaders transform trials into triumphs and setbacks into stepping stones, guiding their teams through the storm with unwavering resolve and a heart committed to a higher cause.

Purposeful leadership is not about avoiding the storm but learning to navigate it with resilience, clarity, and compassion, transforming every challenge into an opportunity for growth and impact

The journey to purposeful leadership is often a complex and demanding one, filled with changes and challenges that test the mettle of any leader. It requires not only a clear vision but also the resilience and adaptability to steer through uncertainty and adversity. Here are key aspects to consider when navigating this path.

Embracing Change as a Constant

Change is an inevitable part of any leadership journey. Whether it's evolving market conditions, organizational restructuring, or shifts in societal expectations, leaders must view change not as a threat but as an opportunity.

Purposeful leaders embrace change with a growth mindset, understanding that it is through change that innovation and progress occur. They remain open to new ideas and perspectives, continuously learning and adapting their strategies to align with evolving circumstances.

Developing Resilience

Challenges, both expected and unforeseen, are a natural component of leadership. Purposeful leaders cultivate resilience—the capacity to recover quickly from difficulties and remain steadfast in their mission.

This resilience is not merely about enduring hardships but about thriving amidst them. It involves maintaining a positive outlook, practicing self-care, and building a support system that includes mentors, peers, and teams who can offer guidance and encouragement.

Maintaining Clarity of Purpose

In the face of change and challenges, it is easy for leaders to lose sight of their core purpose. However, purposeful leadership demands unwavering clarity of purpose—a deep-seated understanding of why one leads and what impact they wish to have.

This clarity acts as a compass, guiding decisions and actions even when the path ahead is uncertain. Leaders who stay connected to their purpose inspire others and create a sense of shared direction and commitment within their teams.

Adaptive Leadership

Purposeful leaders are adaptive leaders. They understand that various circumstances necessitate various strategies. During times of crisis, they may need to be more directive and decisive, while in periods of stability, they might focus on empowering their teams and fostering collaboration.

Adaptive leadership requires emotional intelligence, self-awareness, and the ability to read the context and respond appropriately.

Building and Leveraging a Support Network
No leader can navigate the complexities of change and challenges alone. Purposeful leaders actively build and leverage networks of support, including mentors, advisors, peers, and their own teams.

They seek diverse perspectives, ask for feedback, and are willing to collaborate and share leadership when necessary. This network not only provides practical support but also emotional and psychological sustenance, helping leaders stay grounded and focused.

Leading with Empathy and Compassion

Purposeful leaders understand that change and challenges affect not only them but also their teams and stakeholders. They lead with empathy and compassion, acknowledging the fears and uncertainties that others may be experiencing.

By creating a culture of openness and support, they foster resilience within their teams, encouraging people to voice concerns, share ideas, and contribute to problem-solving.

Continuous Self-Reflection and Growth

Finally, purposeful leaders engage in continuous self-reflection and growth. They regularly assess their own strengths and weaknesses, seek feedback, and commit to personal and professional development. This reflective practice enables them to learn from their experiences, adjust their approaches, and become more effective leaders over time.

navigating change and challenges on the path to purposeful leadership requires more than just skill and intelligence. It demands a deep sense of purpose, a resilient spirit, and a commitment to continuous growth and adaptation.

By embracing these qualities, leaders can not only overcome the obstacles they face but also inspire and guide others toward a shared vision of a better future.

LEADING THROUGH UNCERTAINTY

In the face of uncertainty, purposeful leaders hold firm to their vision, adapt with courage, and lead with empathy, transforming chaos into a journey of growth and discovery. They understand that true leadership is not about having all the answers but about guiding others with clarity and conviction through the unknown, turning each challenge into an opportunity to strengthen their resolve and deepen their collective purpose.

Leading through uncertainty on the path to purposeful leadership requires a balance of vision, adaptability, and empathy. It involves navigating ambiguity with a clear sense of purpose, while being open to change and unforeseen challenges.

Purposeful leaders anchor themselves and their teams with a compelling vision, providing direction even when the way forward is unclear. They communicate this vision consistently, inspiring confidence and resilience in those around them.

Adaptability is crucial. When fresh facts become available, leaders need to be prepared to change course and modify their plans. This flexibility doesn't mean abandoning the mission, but rather finding new ways to achieve it. In times of uncertainty, the ability to make decisions with incomplete information, and to do so with confidence and decisiveness, becomes vital.

Empathy and emotional intelligence are equally important. Leaders need to acknowledge the fears and anxieties of their teams, creating a safe space for open dialogue and support. By being transparent about the challenges faced and the uncertainties ahead, they foster trust and cohesion. This human connection strengthens the resolve of the group, enabling them to move forward together.

Purposeful leadership in uncertain times also requires a commitment to learning and growth. Leaders who approach uncertainty with a learning mindset see challenges as opportunities for innovation and development.

They encourage experimentation and are not afraid of failure, as long as it leads to better understanding and improvement.

leading through uncertainty is about holding steady to a core purpose while being flexible in execution. It's about guiding others with clarity and compassion, making thoughtful decisions amidst ambiguity, and maintaining the courage to forge ahead even when the path is unclear.

RESILIENCE STRATEGIES FOR LEADERS AND TEAMS

Resilience is not the absence of adversity, but the art of rising stronger and more purposeful with each challenge faced. True resilience in leadership lies not in avoiding difficulties, but in transforming them into opportunities for growth, unity, and deeper purpose.

It's the ability to inspire a team to stand firm amidst the storms, to adapt with courage, and to emerge not just intact, but more committed and capable than before.

Resilience is a cornerstone of purposeful leadership, enabling leaders and teams to navigate challenges with strength and determination. A key strategy for fostering resilience is cultivating a growth mindset. Leaders who embrace setbacks as learning opportunities model a way of thinking that encourages continuous improvement rather than fear of failure.

By openly sharing their own experiences with adversity and how they have grown from them, leaders inspire their teams to view challenges as stepping stones to personal and professional growth.

Creating a culture of psychological safety is another vital aspect of building resilience. When team members feel safe to express their ideas, ask questions, and share concerns without fear of judgment, they are more likely to engage fully and contribute to problem-solving.

Leaders can promote this environment by being approachable, actively listening, and valuing diverse perspectives. This trust-based culture not only strengthens the team's ability to respond to adversity but also enhances collaboration and innovation.

Strong interpersonal connections within the team are also crucial for resilience. Leaders should prioritize team-building activities, regular check-ins, and open communication to strengthen these bonds.

When team members feel supported and connected, they are more likely to persevere through difficult times. Additionally, leaders should build and maintain external networks to share experiences and gain insights from other leaders, further enhancing their own resilience.

A sense of shared purpose is fundamental to resilience. Purpose-driven teams are motivated and focused, even in the face of setbacks. Leaders must clearly communicate the organization's mission and how each team member's work contributes to this larger goal. Revisiting this purpose regularly helps the team stay aligned and committed, providing a strong foundation to withstand and recover from challenges.

Promoting self-care and well-being is essential to maintaining resilience. Leaders should encourage their teams to take care of their mental and physical health by providing resources and fostering a culture that prioritizes balance.

This not only prevents burnout but also ensures that team members have the energy and focus needed to tackle complex problems effectively. Leaders should model these behaviors themselves, demonstrating the importance of well-being in sustaining high performance.

Adaptability and flexibility are essential characteristics of resilient teams. Leaders can nurture these qualities by promoting a mindset of experimentation and openness to change.

Encouraging the team to try new approaches and being willing to pivot when necessary prepares them to handle unexpected disruptions. Developing contingency plans and rehearsing responses to various scenarios can also help teams feel more prepared and less overwhelmed when faced with uncertainty.

Effective communication and transparency from leaders play a crucial role in building resilience. During times of uncertainty, clear, honest communication helps reduce anxiety and builds trust. Leaders should keep their teams informed about the organization's direction, changes, and the reasons behind decisions. This transparency fosters a sense of stability and helps teams remain focused and cohesive, even in challenging situations.

Empowering teams to make decisions is another powerful way to build resilience. Leaders should delegate authority and trust their teams to take initiative and make choices within their areas of responsibility.

This empowerment boosts confidence and enables quicker, more effective responses to challenges. Leaders should provide guidance and support while giving their teams the autonomy to act, fostering a sense of ownership and resilience at all levels.

Reflection and learning from experiences are crucial for long-term resilience. After navigating through a difficult situation, leaders should facilitate a debriefing session to discuss what was learned and how the team can improve. This practice of reflecting on experiences, both positive and negative, helps teams build resilience by learning from their past and preparing better for the future.

Recognizing and celebrating progress is essential for maintaining resilience. Acknowledging the hard work and achievements of the team, no matter how small, boosts morale and reinforces a sense of accomplishment.

Celebrations and recognition remind the team of their capability to overcome challenges, providing motivation and strengthening their resolve to continue moving forward.

Resilience is not just about enduring difficulties but about growing stronger and more purposeful through them. By integrating these strategies, leaders can foster a resilient, purpose-driven culture that enables their teams to thrive, even in the face of adversity.

CHAPTER

4

PERSONAL GROWTH AND CONTINUOUS IMPROVEMENT

True leadership is not defined by the destination but by the journey of growth; it is the continuous pursuit of self-improvement that empowers others to rise alongside you.

In the embrace of challenges and the openness to change, a leader transforms not only themselves but also the lives of those they inspire, creating a ripple effect of purpose and progress that transcends the boundaries of individual ambition.

Personal growth and continuous improvement are foundational elements on the path to purposeful leadership. This journey begins with self-awareness, which allows leaders to recognize their strengths and areas for development.

By engaging in reflective practices, leaders can identify their values, beliefs, and motivations, providing clarity on their leadership style and its impact on others.

As leaders commit to lifelong learning, they cultivate a mindset that embraces challenges and views setbacks as opportunities for growth. This approach not only enhances their skills but also inspires those around them to adopt a similar mindset.

Continuous improvement is about seeking feedback and being open to change, understanding that the most effective leaders are those who actively seek to enhance their capabilities and adapt to evolving circumstances.

Mentorship and collaboration play vital roles in this growth process. Purposeful leaders surround themselves with diverse perspectives, learning from the experiences and insights of others. This collaboration fosters a culture of innovation and resilience, essential for navigating the complexities of leadership.

Emphasizing emotional intelligence is also crucial. Purposeful leaders who understand and manage their emotions can build strong relationships, create inclusive environments, and motivate their teams. By modeling vulnerability and authenticity, they encourage others to do the same, strengthening the overall team dynamic.

Setting clear goals and maintaining a vision for the future are essential for purposeful leadership. Leaders who continuously assess their progress and align their actions with their values are more likely to achieve their objectives. This alignment fosters a sense of purpose and fulfillment, not only for the leader but for the entire team.

The journey of personal growth and continuous improvement in leadership is ongoing. It requires dedication, self-reflection, and a commitment to serving others. By embracing this path, leaders can inspire and empower those around them, creating a legacy of purposeful leadership that extends beyond their own achievements.

DEVELOPING YOUR LEADERSHIP SKILLS

Leadership is not defined by titles or positions; it flourishes in the commitment to self-awareness and the courage to serve others. When we lead with purpose, we ignite a collective passion that transcends individual ambitions, turning challenges into opportunities for growth and collaboration.

In the end, the greatest leaders are those who illuminate the path for others, fostering a legacy of empowerment and meaningful change. True leadership is not about wielding authority, but about inspiring purpose; it is the journey of self-discovery that transforms potential into powerful impact.

Developing leadership skills is a vital journey for anyone aspiring to lead with purpose. This process begins with self-awareness, which allows individuals to recognize their strengths and areas for growth. Reflecting on personal values, beliefs, and experiences can provide insight into what kind of leader one wishes to become.

Effective communication is crucial in this development. Leaders must learn to convey their vision clearly and inspire others to work toward common goals.

This involves not only articulating ideas but also actively listening to team members, fostering an environment where everyone feels valued and heard. Building strong relationships within a team encourages collaboration and trust, essential components of purposeful leadership.

Effective leadership is significantly influenced by emotional intelligence. Understanding one's emotions and the emotions of others can enhance decision-making and conflict resolution.

Leaders with high emotional intelligence can empathize with team members, allowing them to navigate challenges more effectively and maintain a positive work environment.

Continuous learning is fundamental to developing leadership skills. Seeking feedback, engaging in professional development opportunities, and embracing challenges as learning experiences can cultivate resilience and adaptability.

Leaders should be open to new perspectives and willing to adjust their approaches when necessary, fostering a culture of growth within their teams.

Mentorship can also provide valuable insights and guidance. Learning from the experiences of others helps aspiring leaders refine their skills and gain different viewpoints on effective leadership strategies. Finding mentors who exemplify the values and behaviors one aspires to embody can offer inspiration and practical advice on navigating the complexities of leadership.

Purpose-driven leadership involves aligning personal values with the goals of the organization. Leaders should strive to create a vision that reflects their principles and motivates others to contribute to a greater cause.

By fostering a sense of purpose, leaders can inspire commitment and passion within their teams, ultimately leading to more meaningful and impactful outcomes.

Through self-awareness, effective communication, emotional intelligence, continuous learning, mentorship, and purpose alignment, individuals can develop their leadership skills on the path to purposeful leadership.

This journey is not only about enhancing one's abilities but also about inspiring others and creating a positive impact in their lives and organizations.

IDENTIFYING KEY SKILLS FOR EFFECTIVE LEADERSHIP

Effective leadership is not defined by authority, but by the ability to inspire growth, foster collaboration, and embrace change, guiding others toward a shared vision with empathy and purpose.

True leadership is the art of weaving together diverse talents into a tapestry of shared purpose, where emotional intelligence ignites trust, strategic vision illuminates the path forward, and adaptability transforms challenges into opportunities for growth.

In this journey, the greatest leaders are those who empower others to shine, understanding that their strength lies not in control, but in nurturing the potential within each individual.

Identifying key skills for effective leadership is crucial on the path to purposeful leadership. Effective leaders possess a combination of attributes that enable them to inspire, motivate, and guide their teams toward achieving common goals.

One fundamental skill is emotional intelligence, which allows leaders to understand their own emotions and the emotions of others. This awareness fosters strong relationships and enhances communication, enabling leaders to navigate conflicts and build a cohesive team.

Another vital skill is effective communication. Leaders must articulate their vision clearly and inspire their teams with compelling narratives. This involves not just speaking but also listening actively, ensuring that team members feel heard and valued. Transparent communication cultivates trust and openness, essential for a thriving work environment.

Strategic thinking is also essential for effective leadership. Leaders need to assess situations critically, anticipate challenges, and develop plans that align with the organization's objectives.

This foresight helps in making informed decisions that can steer the team through uncertainties while remaining focused on long-term goals.

Adaptability is a key skill in today's rapidly changing landscape. Leaders must be willing to adjust their approaches in response to new information or changing circumstances. This flexibility encourages innovation and resilience within the team, allowing them to pivot when necessary.

Strong problem-solving skills are indispensable for leaders. They should be able to analyze complex issues, consider multiple perspectives, and devise effective solutions. This not only helps in overcoming obstacles but also empowers team members to think critically and contribute their ideas.

Fostering a culture of collaboration is crucial. Leaders should encourage teamwork and inclusivity, recognizing the diverse strengths of their team members. By creating an environment where everyone feels empowered to contribute, leaders can harness the collective intelligence of the group, leading to better outcomes.

Effective leadership requires a dedication to lifelong learning. Leaders who prioritize personal and professional growth set an example for their teams. They stay updated on industry trends, seek feedback, and are open to new ideas, demonstrating that learning is a lifelong journey.

identifying and cultivating these key skills—emotional intelligence, effective communication, strategic thinking, adaptability, problem-solving, collaboration, and a commitment to learning—creates a strong foundation for purposeful leadership.

By embodying these attributes, leaders can inspire their teams and navigate the complexities of their roles, ultimately driving their organizations toward success.

CREATING A PERSONAL DEVELOPMENT PLAN

Purposeful leadership is not a destination but a journey of continuous self-discovery and growth, where the true power lies in aligning who you are with the impact you seek to make. It's about embracing the evolving path, nurturing others as you nurture yourself, and transforming every challenge into an opportunity to deepen your purpose and expand your influence.

Creating a personal development plan on the path to purposeful leadership involves a journey of self-discovery, reflection, and intentional growth. It begins with a deep understanding of one's core values, passions, and strengths.

This self-awareness forms the foundation upon which all development is built. By aligning these elements with a vision of leadership that is both authentic and impactful, a leader can begin to chart a path that resonates with their true purpose.

Setting clear and meaningful goals is crucial. These goals should reflect not only professional aspirations but also personal growth areas that contribute to becoming a more empathetic, resilient, and visionary leader. It is important to approach these goals with a sense of curiosity and openness, willing to explore new ideas, embrace challenges, and learn from setbacks.

Continual learning is a key component of the journey. This involves not only acquiring new skills and knowledge but also seeking out diverse perspectives and experiences that broaden one's understanding of the world and the people in it.

Purposeful leaders recognize that growth often comes from stepping outside of comfort zones and engaging in experiences that challenge preconceived notions and expand one's capacity for empathy and innovation.

Building strong, authentic relationships is another essential aspect of this path. Purposeful leaders understand the importance of connecting with others on a deep level, fostering trust, collaboration, and mutual respect.

By actively listening, providing support, and encouraging the growth of those around them, they create a positive and empowering environment that amplifies the collective potential.

Self-reflection is a practice that should be woven into the fabric of a personal development plan. Regularly taking the time to assess progress, celebrate achievements, and identify areas for further growth ensures that the path remains aligned with one's evolving sense of purpose.

It also provides an opportunity to recalibrate and make adjustments as necessary, ensuring that the journey remains dynamic and responsive to both internal and external changes.

The path to purposeful leadership is not about reaching a final destination but about embracing the ongoing process of becoming. It is about striving to lead with integrity, authenticity, and a deep commitment to making a positive difference.

By crafting a personal development plan that is rooted in purpose and driven by a passion for growth, a leader can embark on a journey that is not only fulfilling for themselves but also transformative for those they lead.

MENTORSHIP AND NETWORKING

Leadership is not a solitary path but a tapestry woven from the threads of mentorship and networking. In the embrace of shared wisdom, we discover our purpose; in the support of a community, we find strength.

Each connection we nurture becomes a beacon of inspiration, guiding us to elevate not only ourselves but those who walk alongside us.

As we cultivate relationships rooted in trust and collaboration, we unlock the potential to transform challenges into opportunities and dreams into realities, shaping a future where purposeful leadership lights the way for generations to come.

True leadership is forged through the bonds of mentorship and the strength of a network, where wisdom is shared, values are upheld, and the journey toward purpose inspires others to rise.

Mentorship and networking are fundamental aspects of personal and professional development, especially for those seeking to become purposeful leaders.

As leaders aspire to create meaningful impact within their organizations and communities, the relationships they nurture can provide invaluable guidance, resources, and support.

Mentorship plays a crucial role in this journey. It offers individuals access to seasoned leaders who share insights, wisdom, and strategies for navigating challenges. A mentor not only helps mentees identify their strengths and areas for growth but also provides the necessary support to develop their leadership skills effectively.

The relationship fosters accountability, encouraging mentees to set goals and pursue them with determination. Regular check-ins and constructive feedback from mentors help maintain focus and commitment to personal and professional development.

Beyond career advancement, mentorship also fosters personal growth. Mentors guide mentees in exploring their values, passions, and purpose, helping them align their leadership style with their authentic selves. This deep understanding of personal values can lead to more genuine and impactful leadership.

Networking complements mentorship by facilitating the development of a diverse professional network. Engaging with peers, industry leaders, and influencers opens doors to new opportunities, collaborations, and partnerships that enrich one's leadership journey.

The exchange of ideas and best practices among leaders from various backgrounds can spark innovation and inspire new approaches to challenges. Moreover, a strong network provides access to resources like workshops, seminars, and conferences, essential for staying current in an ever-evolving landscape.

Networking also fosters a sense of community and support. Leaders can share their experiences, challenges, and successes, which cultivates resilience and motivation—qualities vital for purposeful leadership.

In building these connections, leaders can emphasize their values and vision, creating a clear sense of direction for themselves and their teams. Mentors and networks reinforce these values, providing a sounding board for ideas and aspirations.

Creating inclusive spaces is another critical aspect of purposeful leadership. By connecting with individuals from diverse backgrounds, leaders enrich their understanding of different perspectives, fostering an environment where all voices are valued. This inclusivity enhances decision-making and innovation within teams.

A hallmark of purposeful leadership is the commitment to developing others. Leaders who engage in mentorship actively contribute to the growth of their teams, ensuring that future leaders are equipped to succeed. Investing in others not only builds a strong organizational culture but also creates a legacy of leadership that can inspire future generations.

Mentorship and networking are essential to the journey toward purposeful leadership. By leveraging the guidance of mentors and cultivating a strong network, aspiring leaders can acquire the skills, insights, and connections necessary to lead with intention and impact.

Embracing these relationships enriches one's leadership journey and contributes to the growth of others, creating a lasting influence on the leadership landscape for years to come.

THE POWER OF MENTORSHIP IN LEADERSHIP GROWTH

Leadership flourishes in the fertile ground of mentorship, where the seeds of wisdom are sown through shared experiences and guidance. It is in this sacred exchange that aspiring leaders discover their true potential, cultivating not just skills but a profound sense of purpose.

The legacy of a great leader is measured not only by their achievements but by the leaders they inspire, for in lifting others, we illuminate our own path to greatness. True leadership is not born from authority but nurtured through the wisdom of mentorship; it is the shared journey of growth that transforms potential into purpose.

The power of mentorship in leadership growth is profound and multifaceted. Mentorship provides aspiring leaders with invaluable guidance, support, and insights that can shape their journey toward purposeful leadership. It creates an environment where knowledge is shared, experiences are exchanged, and personal development is prioritized.

A mentor acts as a sounding board, offering feedback that can help refine leadership styles and strategies. This relationship fosters a deeper understanding of one's strengths and weaknesses, allowing emerging leaders to navigate challenges with greater confidence.

Through constructive criticism and encouragement, mentors can inspire their mentees to push beyond their comfort zones, fostering resilience and adaptability—qualities essential for effective leadership.

Mentorship encourages networking and relationship building, crucial components of leadership growth. Mentors often introduce their mentees to a broader professional community, expanding opportunities for collaboration and growth. These connections can lead to valuable partnerships and insights that enrich a leader's perspective.

Mentors model behaviors and practices that mentees can emulate. Observing how mentors handle various situations, from conflict resolution to decision-making, provides practical lessons that can be applied in real-world scenarios. This modeling not only imparts skills but also reinforces the importance of ethical leadership and integrity.

The emotional support provided by mentors can also be a significant factor in a mentee's development. Navigating the complexities of leadership can be daunting, and having someone who understands these challenges can alleviate feelings of isolation.

This support fosters a sense of belonging and empowers individuals to pursue their goals with renewed vigor.

A strong catalyst for both professional and personal development is mentoring. It instills a sense of purpose, encourages continuous learning, and reinforces the notion that leadership is not just about authority but about influence and impact.

By embracing mentorship, leaders not only enhance their capabilities but also contribute to the development of future leaders, creating a cycle of growth and inspiration that benefits entire organizations and communities.

In this way, the journey toward purposeful leadership is enriched, guided by the wisdom and experience of those who have walked the path before.

BUILDING A STRONG PROFESSIONAL NETWORK

True leadership is not defined by the titles we hold, but by the connections we cultivate; a strong network transforms aspirations into collective achievements, igniting purpose in every endeavor.

In the tapestry of success, every thread of relationship adds depth and color, reminding us that our greatest impact is forged through collaboration, empathy, and shared vision.

Building a strong professional network is a crucial aspect of developing purposeful leadership. A robust network not only opens doors to new opportunities but also enhances your capacity to influence and inspire others.

This process begins with a genuine commitment to connecting with individuals across various fields and backgrounds.

Engaging with others involves active listening and showing authentic interest in their experiences and insights. This fosters trust and establishes meaningful relationships, which are the foundation of a powerful network.

Attending industry events, joining professional organizations, and participating in community initiatives are excellent ways to expand your circle. These platforms provide opportunities to meet like-minded individuals, share knowledge, and exchange ideas.

Mentorship plays a pivotal role in this journey. Seeking mentors who have achieved what you aspire to can provide invaluable guidance and support.

They can help you navigate challenges, refine your leadership style, and introduce you to other influential figures. Equally, being a mentor to others not only solidifies your knowledge but also positions you as a leader in your field.

Consistency is key in nurturing these relationships. Regular follow-ups, sharing valuable resources, and offering assistance when possible can keep connections alive. Social media platforms, especially LinkedIn, can be powerful tools for maintaining professional ties and showcasing your expertise.

As you build your network, focus on diversity. Engaging with individuals from different industries, cultures, and perspectives enriches your understanding and enhances your leadership capabilities. This diversity can lead to innovative ideas and solutions that you might not have encountered otherwise.

In the realm of purposeful leadership, it's essential to leverage your network not just for personal gain but also to empower others.

Sharing opportunities, recognizing the achievements of others, and facilitating introductions can strengthen your reputation as a leader who truly cares about the growth of those around you. This commitment to mutual support creates a cycle of empowerment that benefits everyone involved.

Building a strong professional network is an ongoing journey that requires time, effort, and sincerity. By investing in relationships and fostering a spirit of collaboration, you can cultivate a network that not only supports your leadership aspirations but also contributes positively to your community and industry.

In this way, you pave the path to becoming a purposeful leader who inspires and drives meaningful change.

MEASURING YOUR IMPACT

True leadership is measured not by the authority one wields, but by the positive impact one inspires in others; it is the legacy of purpose that transforms individuals and ignites collective greatness.

A leader's true power lies in their ability to nurture potential, foster resilience, and cultivate a shared vision that empowers others to rise. As we walk this path, let us remember that our influence shapes not just the present but also the future, crafting a tapestry of interconnected lives that flourish through collaboration and shared purpose.

Measuring your impact on the path to purposeful leadership involves a deep understanding of how your actions, decisions, and values resonate with others. It requires introspection and a commitment to continuous improvement.

To begin, consider the influence you have on your team and organization. Reflect on how your leadership style fosters collaboration, innovation, and trust.

Engaging with team members through open dialogue can provide valuable insights into their perceptions of your leadership. Soliciting feedback helps you understand your strengths and areas for growth. Pay attention to the outcomes of your initiatives; metrics such as team engagement, productivity, and overall morale can serve as indicators of your impact.

It's important to align your leadership goals with the values and mission of your organization. When your actions are consistent with these core principles, you create a more authentic leadership presence. This alignment can foster a culture of purpose, motivating others to pursue their own goals in tandem with the organization's objectives.

Another aspect to consider is the legacy you wish to leave behind. Purposeful leadership is not only about immediate results but also about long-term influence. Think about how your leadership can inspire future generations, and consider what principles you want to instill in those you lead.

Embracing adaptability is key. The path to purposeful leadership is not linear; it often requires navigating challenges and changing circumstances.

By regularly reassessing your impact and being open to change, you can ensure that your leadership remains relevant and effective in achieving meaningful outcomes.

KEY METRICS FOR ASSESSING LEADERSHIP EFFECTIVENESS

True leadership transcends titles and roles; it is the art of fostering connection and igniting potential in others. A leader's effectiveness is measured not by the power they wield, but by the trust they build, the lives they touch, and the legacy of growth they inspire in their team.

Effective leadership is not defined by authority but by the ability to inspire, engage, and uplift those around you, forging a path where every team member grows and thrives.

Assessing leadership effectiveness is crucial for fostering purposeful leadership, as it helps leaders understand their impact and identify areas for growth. Key metrics can be categorized into various dimensions, starting with employee engagement.

High levels of engagement often indicate that a leader is inspiring and motivating their team, creating a positive workplace culture where individuals feel valued and committed to their work.

Another important metric is team performance. This involves evaluating whether a leader's guidance leads to achieving goals and delivering results. Strong performance metrics suggest effective leadership, while underperformance may signal a need for leaders to adjust their strategies or approaches.

Communication effectiveness also plays a pivotal role in leadership assessment. Leaders who communicate clearly and openly tend to foster better relationships within their teams.

Feedback mechanisms, such as surveys or one-on-one meetings, can provide insight into how well leaders convey expectations and listen to their team's concerns.

Leadership adaptability is another critical metric. Purposeful leaders must navigate change and uncertainty while maintaining team morale. Evaluating a leader's ability to pivot and respond to challenges is essential for long-term success. This adaptability can be assessed through team resilience and how well they handle setbacks or changes in direction.

The development of team members is a vital indicator of leadership effectiveness. Leaders who invest in the growth of their team foster an environment of learning and improvement. Metrics can include the number of training opportunities provided, mentorship initiatives, and individual career progression within the team.

Stakeholder feedback is invaluable. Gathering insights from peers, supervisors, and direct reports can provide a well-rounded view of a leader's effectiveness. This 360-degree feedback approach enables leaders to understand how they are perceived and the impact of their actions on others.

By focusing on these metrics, organizations can cultivate purposeful leadership that not only drives performance but also enhances employee satisfaction and fosters a culture of growth and collaboration

GATHERING FEEDBACK AND MAKING ADJUSTMENTS

Leadership is not about unwavering certainty but the courage to evolve. Those who seek feedback not as validation but as a guide, and who adjust their course with humility and purpose, turn every lesson into a legacy.

True leaders grow through the wisdom of others, creating a path where every step, no matter how imperfect, moves toward a greater good.

True leadership is a journey of continual refinement; those who embrace feedback and adapt with humility transform not only themselves but everyone they lead.

Gathering feedback and making adjustments are essential practices for anyone on the path to purposeful leadership. Purposeful leadership is not static; it requires continuous self-assessment and an openness to change. Feedback, both positive and constructive, serves as a mirror, reflecting not only your actions but also their impact on others and the organization.

To effectively gather feedback, it's crucial to create an environment where people feel safe to share their honest perspectives. This can be achieved through regular, open communication and by actively seeking input from a diverse group of stakeholders.

Listening with empathy and without defensiveness allows leaders to understand the nuances of the feedback and its underlying intentions.

Once feedback is received, the next step is to reflect on it deeply. It's important to discern patterns and themes, separating useful insights from noise. Reflection should be followed by a willingness to make necessary adjustments.

This may involve changing one's approach, modifying strategies, or even reevaluating core beliefs and values. Adaptability is key to staying aligned with your purpose and maintaining the trust and respect of those you lead.

Purposeful leadership is a dynamic process. As you grow and learn from feedback, your vision and goals may evolve. Embracing this evolution, and making adjustments accordingly, is what keeps your leadership relevant and impactful.

By integrating feedback into your leadership practice, you demonstrate humility, a commitment to personal growth, and a dedication to serving others with integrity and authenticity.

CONCLUSION

Purposeful leadership is the art of navigating the unknown with conviction, lighting the way not by commanding others to follow, but by empowering them to discover their own light and lead the way forward together.

True leadership is not about the destination, but the courage to journey with purpose, integrity, and the relentless commitment to inspire others to find their own path.

Purposeful leadership is more than just guiding others toward a shared vision; it's about embodying the values, integrity, and passion that inspire others to reach beyond what they thought possible.

It requires a commitment to self-awareness, empathy, and a relentless pursuit of growth, not just for oneself but for the collective good. As leaders, the path is not always straightforward, but it is in navigating the complexities and uncertainties with authenticity and courage that true leadership is forged.

Purposeful leadership demands that we hold ourselves accountable, remain adaptable in the face of change, and maintain an unwavering focus on the impact we wish to create. It is this steadfast dedication to purpose that transforms mere leadership into a legacy that influences, inspires, and empowers others to embark on their own journeys of growth and contribution.

The path to purposeful leadership is not just about reaching a destination; it is about the continuous journey of becoming, learning, and leading with intention, integrity, and a profound sense of purpose.

REFLECTING ON YOUR LEADERSHIP JOURNEY

True leadership is a journey of self-discovery and service, where every challenge becomes a lesson, every setback a stepping stone, and every success an opportunity to uplift others. It's not about the path you've chosen, but the purpose you've embraced that defines your legacy.

Purposeful leadership is not about the titles you hold, but the values you uphold, the challenges you transform into opportunities, and the lives you inspire to reach beyond the ordinary.

Reflecting on your leadership journey involves looking back at the experiences, challenges, and growth you've encountered along the way. It's an opportunity to assess the decisions you've made, the values that have guided you, and the impact you've had on those around you. This reflection allows you to recognize not only your strengths but also areas where you can continue to grow and develop.

On the path to purposeful leadership, it's crucial to consider the motivations that drive you. Purposeful leadership is about more than just achieving goals; it's about leading with intention and aligning your actions with a deeper sense of purpose.

This often involves asking yourself why you lead and what you hope to achieve beyond the immediate outcomes. Purposeful leaders are guided by a vision that transcends personal ambition, focusing on creating a positive impact on their team, organization, and community.

A significant part of this reflection is evaluating how you handle challenges and setbacks.

Leadership is rarely a straightforward journey, and moments of difficulty often reveal the true nature of your leadership style.

Reflect on how you've navigated obstacles, how you've supported and motivated your team through tough times, and how these experiences have shaped your leadership philosophy.

Consider also the relationships you've built along the way. Leadership is deeply relational, and the connections you form with others are a testament to your ability to inspire, influence, and collaborate.

Think about the people who have supported you, the feedback they've given, and how those interactions have influenced your growth as a leader. Reflect on how you've empowered others, encouraged their development, and created an environment where they can thrive.

Purposeful leadership is also about self-awareness and continuous improvement. Reflect on how well you understand your own strengths and weaknesses, and how you've sought out opportunities to learn and grow.

This self-awareness is crucial for adapting your leadership style to different situations and for maintaining authenticity in your interactions.

reflecting on your leadership journey is about recognizing that it's a continuous path, not a destination. It's about being open to change, willing to learn from your experiences, and committed to leading with purpose and integrity.

As you continue on this journey, embrace the lessons learned, celebrate the progress made, and stay true to the values that guide you toward becoming a more effective and purposeful leader.

THE ONGOING PATH TO PURPOSEFUL LEADERSHIP

Purposeful leadership transcends titles and authority; it is the art of cultivating trust, nurturing potential, and inspiring others to see beyond limitations. It is about standing steadfast in values, guiding with empathy, and transforming every setback into a testament of resilience and growth.

True leaders do not merely light the path—they ignite the spark within others, enabling them to illuminate their own way forward and together, build a future that resonates with shared purpose and collective strength.

Purposeful leadership is not about leading others to follow, but about empowering them to rise beyond, transforming challenges into stepping stones, and crafting a legacy that breathes life into the greater good.

The ongoing path to purposeful leadership is a journey marked by self-awareness, empathy, and a commitment to serving others. It begins with understanding one's own values and vision, and aligning them with the broader goals of the organization or community. This alignment fosters authenticity, which is crucial for inspiring and motivating others.

Purposeful leadership is not about exerting control or authority; it is about guiding and supporting others in their own growth.

It requires active listening and a deep sense of empathy to understand the needs and aspirations of those you lead. This understanding helps create an environment where individuals feel valued and empowered to contribute their best.

Building trust is essential. It involves being consistent in actions and decisions, showing integrity, and being transparent, especially in challenging situations. Trust lays the foundation for strong relationships and collaboration, which are vital for a thriving team or organization.

Resilience is another key aspect. Purposeful leaders face setbacks and challenges with a mindset of learning and adaptation.

They view obstacles as opportunities for growth and innovation, rather than as barriers to success. This resilience not only helps leaders navigate their own path but also inspires others to persevere.

Continuous learning and self-reflection are fundamental to staying on the path of purposeful leadership. Leaders must remain open to new perspectives and be willing to adapt their approaches as they evolve and as circumstances change. This adaptability ensures that they remain relevant and effective in a constantly changing world.

purposeful leadership is a commitment to a higher calling. It's about making a positive impact, fostering growth, and creating a legacy that transcends personal achievement. It's an ongoing path that requires dedication, humility, and an unwavering focus on the well-being of others and the greater good.

APPENDICES

RECOMMENDED READING AND RESOURCES

To deepen your understanding of purposeful leadership, consider exploring a variety of books, articles, and online courses that provide valuable insights and strategies.

Key texts include "Leaders Eat Last" by Simon Sinek, which emphasizes the importance of creating a supportive team culture, and "Dare to Lead" by Brené Brown, which focuses on vulnerability and trust in leadership.

Resources like Harvard Business Review articles and TED Talks offer diverse perspectives on leadership challenges and best practices.

Online platforms such as Coursera and LinkedIn Learning provide courses tailored to developing leadership skills, ranging from emotional intelligence to conflict resolution.

LEADERSHIP ASSESSMENT TOOLS

Utilizing assessment tools can help individuals and teams evaluate their leadership capabilities and identify areas for improvement.

Tools like the 360-Degree Feedback, which gathers insights from peers, subordinates, and superiors, can provide a comprehensive view of leadership effectiveness.

The Myers-Briggs Type Indicator (MBTI) and the DiSC Profile offer valuable insights into personality types and communication styles, helping leaders understand their strengths and how to leverage them effectively.

Regularly using these tools can facilitate growth and enhance team dynamics by fostering open communication and self-awareness.

ACTION PLAN TEMPLATE FOR PERSONAL AND TEAM GROWTH

Creating a structured action plan is essential for implementing purposeful leadership strategies. Start by defining clear, measurable goals for both personal and team development.

Include sections for identifying strengths and weaknesses, setting timelines, and determining necessary resources.

Integrate checkpoints to review progress and adjust strategies as needed. Encourage team members to collaborate in developing this plan, fostering ownership and commitment to shared objectives.

By following a structured approach, leaders can effectively navigate their journey toward personal and team growth, ensuring alignment with overarching organizational goals.

ACKNOWLEDGMENTS

In the journey toward purposeful leadership, I am deeply grateful for the unwavering support and inspiration I have received from many remarkable individuals.

I would like to extend my heartfelt thanks to my mentors, whose guidance has shaped my understanding of leadership and empowered me to embrace my unique path. Your insight and support have been truly priceless.

To my colleagues and peers, your collaboration and insights have enriched my perspective and challenged me to grow. Together, we have navigated the complexities of leadership, and I am thankful for the camaraderie and shared experiences that have made this journey rewarding.

I also want to acknowledge the countless authors, thinkers, and leaders whose works have illuminated the way forward. Your contributions have ignited my passion for purposeful leadership and provided a solid foundation upon which I have built my understanding.

Finally, I express my deepest appreciation to my family and friends for their unwavering support and belief in my vision. Your love and encouragement have been a source of strength, reminding me of the importance of leading with purpose and integrity.

This journey is as much yours as it is mine, and I look forward to continuing this path together.

ABOUT THE AUTHOR

Scott E. Salsbury is a distinguished author and thought leader in the field of leadership development, best known for his groundbreaking book, *Path to Purposeful Leadership*. With a career spanning over two decades, Salsbury combines practical experience and academic insight to guide aspiring and seasoned leaders alike in discovering their authentic leadership styles.

His approach emphasizes the importance of purpose, emotional intelligence, and ethical decision-making in fostering effective leadership.

In addition to his writing, Salsbury is a sought-after speaker and consultant, working with organizations to cultivate leadership capabilities at all levels.

His engaging workshops and seminars have inspired countless individuals to embrace a more intentional and purposeful approach to their leadership journeys. Salsbury's work continues to impact the leadership landscape, empowering others to lead with clarity, vision, and purpose.

www.ingramcontent.com/pod-product-compliance
Lightning Source LLC
Chambersburg PA
CBHW052151220526
45471CB00004B/1625